REMEMBERING
THE FORGOTTEN
GOD

The Search For Truth
In The Modern World

REMEMBERING
THE FORGOTTEN
GOD

R. E. Simmons, III

Atticus Press & Company, Inc.

1993

CONTENTS

This book is dedicated to my family, the most important people in my life. To my parents: Richard and Lynne; my brothers, sisters, and their spouses: Marion and Pat, Kip and Debbie, Catherine and John, Missy, Paul and Wendy, and David; and finally my nephews and niece: Drew, Kelly, Charlie, Whit, and Daniel.

People are fated to choose for or against God, though many go through life caring nothing about this eternal decision. This same man who spends so many days and nights in rage and despair for the loss of office, or for some imaginary insult to his honor, is the very one who knows . . . that he will lose all by death.

Blaise Pascal

Foreword

A number of years ago *Encyclopædia Britannica* published a fifty-five volume series entitled *The Great Books of the Western World*. This series presented the most important ideas scholars and intellectuals have considered and investigated over the course of recorded history.

The longest essay was on God.

When noted philosopher and author Mortimer Adler, co-editor of the series, was asked why this would be so, he replied, "It is because more consequences for life follow from that one issue than from any other."

I believe Dr. Adler's forthright assessment of history and God's place in it to be correct. History is driven by each generation's quest to find meaning and purpose in life, by each individual's relationship with God. The major issues of life—whether they involve personal values such as love and happiness or political mandates such as war and peace—are understood with the greatest clarity only after the question of God's existence is placed in its proper context.

Honesty is absolutely necessary in any search for God. Ravi Zacharias, a contemporary philosopher and theologian who lectures worldwide, tells the story of the man who woke up one morning and told his family that he was dead. His family thought they would have to endure this silliness for just a little while; but each morning he would get up and ask them if they were convinced yet that he was dead. He then began to broadcast this delusion at the office and in public. Finally, his family and friends concluded, he needed medical attention.

He went to several psychiatrists, but they could not help him. His family finally had him meet with a battery of neurologists who intended to demonstrate to him that only living people bleed. After hours of witnessing conclusive medical evidence, the man weakly admitted to the physicians, "I guess you are right, only living people bleed." As soon as the man uttered these words, one of the doctors whipped out a pin he had hidden in his coat and stuck it in the man's arm. The blood began to flow, and in astonishment he said, "Great scott, look at that. I guess dead people bleed, too, after all."

Dr. Zacharias tells this story of the "dead" man to reveal how stubborn and close-minded we all can be. As a result of our biases and our selfish needs, we often refuse to embrace new ideas. And, worse yet, we refuse even to acknowledge the time-tested truths of our forebears. We become just like the "dead" man: regardless of the evidence that might be presented, we will not be swayed.

To reach a conclusion concerning the existence or nonexistence of God is the worthiest and the most important pursuit of humanity. The pages which follow contain what I have discovered in my own personal search for God and for truth. I will be the first to acknowledge that any attempt to remove all doubt as to His existence would be futile. Yet, it is important to point out that just as one cannot absolutely prove His existence, neither can one absolutely disprove it. In the words of Alfred Lord Tennyson, "nothing worthy proving can be proven, nor yet disproven."

Ultimately, belief or disbelief in God's existence will remain a matter of individual faith—a faith founded on reason as well as emotion, a faith based on the weight of historical precedent, a faith driven by the force of logic and fact and one's own individual experience of the world. This is what I have attempted to do in this work: to present my experience and ask you to remember yours. I have appealed throughout to the writings and words of others, words which have refined, challenged, and ultimately supported my own personal faith. I believe that if you are intellectually and emotionally honest, you, too, will find support in history and in experience. God, although frequently forgotten by man, has not once forgotten mankind.

Richard Earl Simmons, III

August 1992

Once blasphemy against God was the greatest blasphemy; but God died . . . .

Friedrich Nietzsche

The Existence of God

John Stott, one of the preeminent theologians of our day, insists that the greatest of all human tragedies is that men and women go through life with indifference towards the existence of God. Indeed, history suggests that people spend a lifetime searching for knowledge, for wealth, for pleasure, and for love, while seldom taking even a moment to determine if God is real. I have often wondered how many people actually spend time searching for God, and, of those who do, how many come to a rational, defensible conclusion to which they are then willing to commit their lives.

Where do you start the search? How do you search for an invisible being? Obviously, there is no way that finite man can ever find this supposed infinite, invisible God. Unless, that is, this infinite, invisible God steps forward and reveals Himself. If He cannot be seen, might He not have left a visible sign that can clearly be discerned and remembered?

Very early in my own search, I reached the conclusion that either God exists or does not exist. There is no third option. I find, however, that many people I meet are content to live out their lives either denying this reality or choosing not to consider the implications of its truth. It is possible, of course, to sidestep the issue whenever one is confronted with it; and I suppose some will even suggest that this constitutes an option. In that denial, however, one chooses to live a life of intellectual laziness in a spiritual limbo. Such a person may get by just fine, but he will never live a life of harmony and peace because he is not being totally honest with himself. Either God exists or does not exist; there is no third option.

These alternative belief systems—*theism* and *atheism*—offer radically different perspectives on life. They are not just two separate views of life; they are opposing, mutually exclusive views, delivering opposite conclusions about the meaning of life and our existence as human beings. A person who is searching for an answer to the question of God's existence must take time to fully understand the logical conclusions derived from *both* theism and atheism. This understanding will provide light for the search. Ultimately, the perspective which is true will be consistent with the real world and the perspective which is untrue will present a view of life that simply does not fit in with the universe.

An atheist is an individual who is convinced that God does not exist and that all notions of God are but myths. When you sift through the philosophical beliefs of the atheist, you will recognize that atheists offer a coherent world view and are completely rational in their thinking. The atheist intellectuals cited in this chapter are authorities in their respective fields and, consequently, the conclusions they draw may be counted on as representative of the atheistic point of view. Quite frankly, the atheist is more intellectually interesting and honest than the majority of well-educated, successful men and women in the world who spend their lives in denial, dodging the decision. The atheist realizes, at least, that a decision must be made.

Atheism and Morality

In modern thought, the prevailing viewpoint within intellectual circles has been that there is no absolute moral code. As situations change and environments are altered, morality will also inevitably change. For instance, a man believes that abortion is categorically wrong—until, that is, the day his fifteen-year-old daughter reveals she is pregnant. Assume this revelation forces him to radically rethink his position and ultimately leads to a change in his convictions. Although the fundamental and extraordinarily difficult issues surrounding abortion have not changed, his personal response to the situation has.

If the appropriate response to any given situation is determined solely by one's shifting perspective and is a result of individual circumstance, then morality remains in constant flux. This position, often referred to as *situational ethics*, has been embraced by more than just the intellectual elite. George Barna, a statistical sociologist, has recently concluded extensive research and polling of the American people, the results of which have been documented in his book *What Americans Believe*. Barna states emphatically that the results reflect that a majority of Americans believe there is no such thing as absolute truth and, consequently, there is no absolute moral standard for people to live by.

If this is true, we cannot say anything is absolutely right or wrong. When confronted with crucial social issues such as pornography, rape, or drug use, there is neither right nor wrong, only a personal, potentially situational opinion on the issue.

This equivocal view of morality has its roots in an atheistic perspective of life. When a society removes God from moral consideration, morality and ethics in that society become relative. If there is no transcendent and authoritative reality—no God—there can be no absolute values in life, for, without God, no finite authority is able to establish absolute right and wrong. With no God to provide a moral framework, human beings are compelled to base their behavior on desire, utility, or expedience.

Alexander Solzhenitsyn not only understood the theoretical implications of the atheistic view of morality—situational ethics—he suffered under it in the former Soviet Union. Recognizing that communism is rooted in atheism,

Solzhenitsyn writes:

> Communism has never concealed the fact it rejects all absolute concepts of morality. It scoffs at good and evil as indisputable categories. Morality is relative. Depending on circumstances, any act, including the killing of thousands, could be good or bad. It is considered awkward to use such words as good and evil, and yet if we are deprived of these concepts, what are we left with? We will decline to the status of animals.

Solzhenitsyn is describing a society where there is no absolute right and wrong because the society is ruled by men who do not believe there is a God who gives us a moral framework. Taking this view to its logical conclusion, the atheist must admit that ideas such as justice, kindness, cruelty, and honor, which are rooted in some notion of good and evil, right and wrong, are meaningless.

B. F. Skinner, a highly influential twentieth century psychologist, a man who emphatically rejected a belief in God, had much to say about morality. He believed the moral life of humanity to be a delusion; he saw morality as being a restriction on man's freedom and a hindrance to the survival of the human race. For Skinner, all human behavior is determined and conditioned by environmental influences; there are no truly independent actions or behaviors.

Aldous Huxley, an atheistic novelist, demonstrated in his work the absurdity of an absolute moral code in a godless universe. In his brilliant novel, *Brave New World*, Huxley pictures a society that turns traditional morality on its head: fidelity and faithfulness become evil and dirty, while promiscuity and intrigue become good and virtuous.

In 1948, the philosopher Bertrand Russell, an outspoken atheist, participated in a debate with F. C. Copleston, broadcasted on the BBC, concerning the question of the existence of God. As the debate progressed, the two men addressed the moral argument for the existence of God. Copleston asked Russell how he distinguished between good and evil.

Russell:	I don't have any justification any more than I have when I distinguish between yellow and blue. What is my justification for distinguishing between yellow and blue? I can see they are different.
Copleston:	You distinguish between yellow and blue by seeing them; so you distinguish good and evil by what faculty?
Russell:	By my feelings.

Mr. Russell clearly believed that mankind has not been given a transcendent moral imperative. Therefore, because there is no God, ethical decisions should be made by one's feelings. A modern saying that best expresses this system of morality is "if it feels good, do it."

Whose feelings will determine right and wrong in a community? In Nazi Germany, it was Adolph Hitler's "feelings," for Hitler truly "felt" that the extinction of the Jews was right and good. He considered Aryans the inheritors of the future and Jews as an inferior species unworthy of preservation. Who were we in the Allied countries to say these "feelings" were evil and wrong?

This issue was addressed at the Nuremberg trials as questions arose over what laws should be used to judge the Nazis. Before the trials began, the Allies had prepared a Charter Tribunal consisting of the rules of procedure, the rules of evidence, and the laws under which the Nazis would be prosecuted. The Nazi defendants claimed that they were being tried by *ex post facto* laws and several authorities in international law criticized the Allied judges for the same reasons. The Nazis on trial logically appealed to the fact that they consistently followed the mandates of their country and government and that their actions were in obedience to the laws in effect at the time. They argued that they could not be convicted simply because their behavior deviated from the contrary value system of their conquerors.

The chief counsel for the United States at the Nuremburg trials, Robert H. Jackson, appealed to permanent, transcultural values. He appealed to a law beyond the law, a universal law. He said that a system of ethics must point beyond itself—it has to be transcendental and its basis cannot rest within the finite world. Otherwise, how could one, in good faith, say that the Nazis were wrong in their actions?

Thus, a real dilemma exists when mankind lives in a moral vacuum. Charles Colson, a contemporary Christian essayist, echoes this thought:

> Everyone is clamoring for ethics, we want more ethics. Someone recently gave $35 million to Harvard Business School to set up a chair on ethics. The problem is whose ethics? There is no foundation upon which to rest a set of ethics, and that is why Harvard, for two years, has been trying to figure how to spend the $35 million. All they have been able to do is hire one professor, and they have yet to design a curriculum because they can't agree on whose ethics they are going to teach.

God and Morality

The existence of God brings to this moral dilemma a completely different perspective. The theist believes that God gives to man a permanent, absolute, transcendental law. Morality is not determined by the feelings and opinions of a plurality of men; rather, it is God who determines what is right and wrong, what is good and what is evil. Consequently, terms such as justice, kindness, cruelty, and honor have meaning.

The theist recognizes that God has given to man a moral law for man's own benefit. Moral law, the theist believes, is designed to provide a standard by which individuals and societies should make decisions, to produce order and social harmony, and to prevent chaos and disorder from destroying society.

Soon after C. S. Lewis, professor of Renaissance and Medieval English at Cambridge, was converted from atheism to Christianity, he shared how he had made what he called a second discovery—he had experienced, he said, the presence of evil. As an atheist, this brilliant man believed that good and evil were meaningless words. Yet, once Lewis was convinced of the existence of God, he quickly recognized the presence of an absolute moral law which had been handed down by God, and he observed that evil was no longer a meaningless word but rather a stark reality in life.

The Value of Human Life

Have you ever wondered why, in our vast world, human rights and human life are important to some and of no importance to others? It is only recently, for example, that United States politicians have come to recognize human rights as an important issue. They speak out loudly when traveling to countries where basic human rights are violated and human beings are expendable.

Human life is cheap if there is no God. In a Godless universe, man is nothing more than a mass of chemicals. Frederich Nietzsche saw man as an animal; B. F. Skinner reduced man to the status of machine; and the famous French existentialist Jean Paul Sartre regarded man as nothing more than a "useless passion."

When Skinner was asked how he could regard man as nothing more than a machine that responds mechanically to stimuli in accordance with prior patterns of reinforcement, he rejoined by openly mocking the dignity of man. In effect, he said that he was glad to see the riddance of the sacredness of man, "his abolition has been long overdue." In *Beyond Freedom and Dignity*, Skinner insists that man's behavior is conditioned merely by the environment, that freedom is an illusion, and that there is no reason to regard human beings as anything other than a product of nature. When you cut through all of Skinner's rhetoric, he is saying there is no qualitative difference between men and maggots. We are all merely nature's products.

Before his conversion to theism, Mortimer Adler believed man to be nothing more than a sophisticated animal. For this reason, he said, "there is no logical reason to treat mankind differently from any other animal.

Therefore, to exploit minorities or to exterminate the homeless could not be condemned any more than the killing of steers in a slaughterhouse."

Though Adler's assertion may sound heartless, he is logically correct. Man, the most developed of all animals yet nonetheless still an animal, deserves no special privileges. Why should the majority, the momentary status quo, stand up for the minority when they are treated like dogs if men are indeed no different from dogs? Why not simply allow the hungry multitudes in Third World countries to starve to death in order to decrease the surplus population of the world? Why condemn rape when throughout the animal kingdom males force themselves indiscriminately upon females? Why should any human being be given special treatment by any other human being?

In a godless universe, the law of natural selection rules; it is every man for himself. Let the strong survive and the weak decline.

In the October 3, 1983 issue of *Time* magazine there was an essay entitled "Thinking Animal Thoughts." In the article, *Time* examined the differences between animal life and human life. The article concluded:

> If human beings assume that they were created in the image of God,
> it is not difficult for them to see the vast and qualitative distance
> between themselves and the lesser orders of creation. The Bible
> teaches that man has dominion over the fish of the sea, the fowl of
> the air, the cattle and every creeping thing. Perhaps the rise of the
> animal rights movement is a symptom of a more secular and self-
> doubting spirit. The human difference is known, to some, as the
> immortal soul, an absolute distinction belonging to man and woman
> alone, not to the animal. The soul is the human pedigree—presum-
> ably the dispensation to slay and eat any inferior life that crosses the
> path. But in a secular sense, how is human life different from animal
> life? Intelligence? Some pygmy chimps and even lesser creatures
> are as intelligent as, say, a severely retarded child; if it is not permis-
> sible to kill a retarded child, why kill the animals?

In a godless universe, man has no intrinsic value. There is no real difference in human life and animal life.

In September 1990, I had a most interesting discussion with an intelligent graduate student who could not subscribe to a theistic view of life. We discussed why human life was regarded as being sacred. I argued that we naturally recognize the value of human life because this sacredness was God given. He on the other hand, argued that it is a result of being culturally conditioned from birth.

I then asked him a simple question. "Are you telling me that human beings are really nothing more than a mass of chemicals, with no intrinsic value?"

"That's right," he responded.

I then asked one final question. "Then Hitler was not wrong in disposing of that large mass of chemicals during the Holocaust?"

"No, Hitler was not 'wrong.'"

As soon as these words left his mouth, he began to laugh nervously. He obviously could not believe what he had just said. In attempting to be logically consistent with his atheistic world view, he ended up surprising himself. It was not a pleasant surprise.

The Dignity of Man

Theism recognizes that life was handed down from a higher source and therefore all men and women are special creatures of great value. The theist recognizes that it is the mind of God that stands behind our existence; it is the mind of God that created and continues to shape our existence. It is God who chose to design all human beings like Himself. In effect, all people—men and women, black and white, from the east and from the west—have inherited His traits of intelligence and personality, the ability to reason, to love, and to communicate. For this reason, human life has a value that transcends animal life. This explains why protecting human rights and standing against human cruelty and abuse is so vitally important to the theist and to theistic societies.

In his book, *In Search of Dignity*, R. C. Sproul has properly described the vital link between God and the dignity of man: it is because God has assigned worth to mankind that human dignity is established. This dignity is derived from and is dependent on the fact that God values his people. It is because mankind bears the image of God that he enjoys such an exalted rank in nature. Consequently, man's origin is significant—his destiny is significant—*he* is significant.

Dr. John Hallowell, a professor of Political Science at Duke University, concludes his *Main Currents in Modern Political Thought* with a powerful warning:

> Having lost sight of the fact that God created all men in His image, the modern world has no basis for believing that all men are equal. We are left without any rational means of defending the belief in individual equality. The crisis in which we find ourselves is the culmination of modern man's progressive attempt to deny the existence of a transcendent or spiritual reality and of his progressive failure to find meaning and salvation in some wholly immanent conception of reality. The solution lies in a society that intellectually and spiritually is God-centered rather than man-centered.

Charles Colson has described the former Soviet Union as a nation committed to the eradication of the practice of religion. The leaders of the old Soviet Union declared God to be officially dead. However, the death of God ultimately spells the death of what it means to be truly human. It is only logical that if worth is not God given, it must be established by man. A government with an atheistic world view will therefore treat man as an object whose worth is determined solely by his usefulness to society. For this reason, such a government will subject its people to whatever will achieve its objectives, whether it be through means of aggression, torture, or . . . genocide.

The dissolution of the monolithic Soviet Union was, in large measure, a result of the inhumane manner in which the government carried out its policies. In the end, the mood of the Soviet people was one of malaise and boredom; life had been drained out of them. When a nation is unified, it is strong. The Soviet

Union lost its strength when the people, after decades of dehumanizing treatment from their government, recognized that communism had failed them and would continue to fail them. In the end, the dignity of man prevailed.

In comparing an atheistic assessment of man with the theistic convictions displayed in the Godly actions of Mother Theresa, a stark contrast is observed. For many years, this saintly woman has provided shelter and help for the homeless, the sick, and the poor, all living out their lives in pain, fear, and loneliness. Many times she is asked why care for those who are doomed anyway? She responds, "They are created by God; they deserve to die with dignity." She clearly believes that every person is precious, a preciousness formulated by God's creative act.

Philip Yancy, a contemporary Christian journalist, relates a powerful story in the January 13, 1989 issue of *Christianity Today*. Yancy decided he would like to interview a pastor about whom he had read in a church newsletter. This pastor was also a psychologist and a counselor, a calling he was led to through an extraordinary experience in World War II.

The experience concerned the liberation of Dachau concentration camp, and Yancy was determined to learn more about it. Yancy recalls his visit and conversation with the pastor.

It was a blustery Chicago day, and I sat hunched in a wool sweater next to a hissing radiator . . . . The pastor looked off to his right, seeming to focus on a blank space on the wall. He was silent for at least a minute. His eyes moved back and forth rapidly, as if straining to fill in the scene from forty years before. Finally he spoke, and for the next twenty minutes he recalled the sights, the sounds and the smells—especially the smells—that greeted his units as they marched through the gates of Dachau.

For weeks the soldiers had heard wild rumors about the camps, but believing it to be war propaganda, they gave little credence to such rumors. Nothing prepared them, and nothing could possibly prepare them, for what they found inside.

"A buddy and I were assigned to one boxcar. Inside were human corpses, stacked in neat rows, exactly like firewood. The

Germans, ever meticulous, had planned out the rows—alternating the heads and feet, accommodating different sizes and shapes of bodies.

"Our job was like moving furniture. We would pick up each body—so light!—and carry it to a designated area. Some fellows couldn't do this part. They stood by the barbed wire fences, retching.

"I couldn't believe it the first time we came across a person in the pile still alive. But it was true. Incredibly, some of the corpses weren't corpses. They were human beings. We yelled for doctors, and they went to work on these survivors right away.

"I spent two hours in that boxcar, two hours that for me included every known emotion: rage, pity, shame, revulsion—every negative emotion, I should say. They came in waves, all but the rage. It stayed, fueling our work. We had no other emotional vocabulary for such a scene.

"After we had taken the few survivors to a makeshift clinic, we turned our attention to the SS officers in charge of Dachau, who were being held under guard in a bunkhouse. Army Intelligence had set up an interrogation center nearby. It was outside the camp, and to reach it you had to walk down a ravine through some trees. The captain asked for a volunteer to escort a group of twelve SS prisoners to the interrogation center, and Chuck's hand shot right up.

"Chuck was the loudest, most brash, most volatile soldier in our unit. He stood about five-feet, four-inches tall, but he had overly long arms so that his hands hung down around his knees like a gorilla's. He came from Cicero, a suburb of Chicago, known mainly for its racism and its association with Al Capone. Chuck claimed to have worked for Capone before the war, and not one of us doubted it.

"Well, Chuck grabbed a submachine gun and prodded the group of SS prisoners down the trail. They walked ahead of him with their hands locked back behind their heads, their elbows sticking out on either side. A few minutes after they disappeared into the trees, we heard the rattling burp of a machine gun in three long burst of fire. We all ducked; it could have been a German sniper in the woods. But soon Chuck came strolling out, smoke still curling from the tip of his weapon. 'They all tried to run away,' he said, with a kind of leer."

I asked if anyone reported what he did or took disciplinary action. The pastor laughed, and then he gave me a get-serious-this-is-war look.

"No, and that's what got to me. It was on that day that I felt called by God to become a pastor. First, there was the horror of the corpses in the boxcar. I could not absorb such a scene. I did not even know such Absolute Evil existed. But when I saw it, I knew beyond doubt that I must spend my life serving whatever opposed such Evil—serving God.

"Then came the Chuck incident. I had a nauseating fear that the captain might call on me to escort the next group of SS guards, and an even more dreadful fear that if he did, I might do the same as Chuck. The beast that was within those guards was also within me."

I could not coax more reminiscing from the pastor that day. Either he had probed the past enough, or he felt obligated to move on to our own agenda. But before we left the subject entirely, I asked a question that, as I look back now, seems almost impudent.

"Tell me," I asked, "after such a cosmic kind of call to the ministry—confronting the great Evil of the century—how must it feel to fulfill that call by sitting in this office listening to middle-class yuppies like me ramble on about our personal problems?"

His answer came back quickly, as if he had asked himself that question many times.

"I do see the connection," he said. "Without being melodramatic, I sometimes wonder what might have happened if a skilled, sensitive person had befriended the young, impressionable Adolf Hitler as he wandered the streets of Vienna in his confused state. The world might have been spared all that bloodshed—at Dachau. I never know who might be sitting in that chair you're occupying right now.

"And even if I end up spending my life with 'nobodies,' I learned in the boxcar that there's no such thing. Those corpses with a pulse were as close to nobodies as you can get: mere skeletons wrapped in papery skin. But I would have done anything to keep those poor, ragged souls alive. Our medics stayed up all night to save them; some in our company lost their lives to liberate them. There are no 'nobodies.' I learned that day in Dachau what 'the image of God' in a human being is all about."

Ask yourself a very simple question. Do you believe that you—and all other human beings—are unique in a way that cannot be explained by the idea that you are a sophisticated animal or an elaborate machine? Do your family members and all the people in your life have value beyond the emotional, physical, and financial support you get from them? The only way human life can be extolled and held sacred is if God in His divine wisdom created mankind as a reflection of Himself.

Love Without God

"I love you."

Those three words are often difficult to say and even more difficult to understand. And to complicate matters, in today's culture love is often nothing more than a cheap four-letter word used to describe our feelings toward ice cream, a good movie, or a popular rock song. R. C. Sproul has said that as a buzzword, overused and abused, the word *love* faces a future of becoming almost empty of meaning.

Even so, the sound of the word—in the proper context and in the appropriate setting—is still able to cast a spell on the human heart like no other phenomenon. Victor Frankl, a Jewish writer who survived the concentration camps of the Holocaust, has said that love is the ultimate and highest goal to which all human beings aspire. To love and to be loved is the deepest of all yearnings of the human heart. It is, therefore, not surprising that we experience the greatest joy in this life when we love . . . *truly* love.

But where does love fit in a world where God does not exist? Once again, we must turn to the words and deeds of the atheist. The atheist, by virtue of his beliefs, is forced to live an existence where love does not have a meaningful place. As B. F. Skinner has concluded, "love is an illusion."

The French existentialist, Jean Paul Sartre painted a very bleak picture of love. In his book *Nausea*, Sartre gives life to a character named Roquentin, who speaks of his disgust at the way in which a man and a woman are behaving toward one another. Roquentin's disgust stems from his recognition of the absurdity of the very idea of love in a godless universe.

Aldous Huxley was even more critical of the idea of love. "Of all the worn, smudged, dog-eared words in our vocabulary, love is surely the grubbiest, smelliest, slimiest. Bawled from a million pulpits, lasciviously crooned through hundreds of loud speakers, it has become an outrage to good taste and decent feeling, an obscenity which one hesitates to pronounce."

More recently, in the popular movie "Wall Street," Oliver Stone casts Michael Douglas as the soulless Wall Street magnate Gordon Gekko. Gekko lives without compassion and morals, maniacally driven by his lust for power and wealth. When commenting on love and human relationships, he laughs and remarks, "I am smart enough not to buy into the oldest myth running— love. It is fiction created by people to keep them from jumping out of windows."

The atheist, then, is forced to renounce the mystery of love, yet must explain that which humanity recognizes to be a true phenomenon. He, therefore, matter-of-factly, as Dr. William Kilpatrick, professor of psychology at Boston College, tells us, explains love away as follows:

- •Love is a sublimation of the sex drive produced in the right brain hemisphere.
- •Love is a matter of stimulus and response conditioned by family patterns of reward.
- •Love is the inherited drive to preserve the genetic pool.

Dr. Kilpatrick goes on to say that to understand love in a godless world we are "encouraged to forget about Romeo and Juliet, and to think rather in terms of some new study of the sexual behavior of two thousand couples in the Midwest, or some observations on the mating patterns of chimpanzees, or to re-order our understanding along the lines of some such formula as, 'she is the mother that he always wished to possess.'"

Love is explained away by atheists as a chemical reaction, a biological drive, an animal instinct, a conditioned phenomenon.

The Reality of Love

Dr. Francis Schaeffer, philosopher, scholar, and author of several seminal works of theology, introduces us to the parable of the two young lovers on the Left Bank of Paris who fall in love and then weep because they do not believe that love truly exists. Schaeffer goes on to describe what he would say to these young lovers if he were to meet them: "At this moment you understand something real about the universe. Though your system may say love does not exist, your own experience shows that it does. Though these youngsters do not believe in a personal God, for a fleeting moment, they have touched the existence of true personality in their love. This indeed is an objective reality, and no mere illusion."

Susan Macaulay, in her book *How to Be Your Own Selfish Pig*, shares the true story of Philippe and Françoise, two bright and sophisticated students at the Sorbonne University in Paris. One day the two meet, romance blossoms, and they begin living together during the school year.

When their studies end, the lovers are perplexed over what to do next. It is more *convenient* for them to separate, so they part and go their separate ways.

Phillipe tries to push aside his feelings for Françoise by employing the concepts he learned in his philosophy classes at school. *Love is an illusion,* he reasons. *These feelings I have are temporary and are a result of my hormones. Other women will come along to replace Françoise.*

As the months go by, Phillipe and Françoise cannot forget each other. The sexual relationships they experience with others seem empty. They pursue lives that they believe will provide them excitement and satisfaction, but find that the theory they believe in is not working for them. They finally come back together.

Mrs. McCaulay first met Phillipe at the L'Abri School in Switzerland where his confusion eventually lead him. Phillipe could not understand why it was so difficult to live without genuine love and commitment in life. He acknowledged that he never realized how his atheistic ideas about life were draining it of its joy:

"I have always believed that the human being was the result of chance. We are like machines doing what we are programmed to do by our genes and instincts and hormones. This means that I cannot make choices; my genetic program is running me. I cannot really love. A computer can't love! Beauty has no meaning. Love relationships are a farce, an illusion!"

For Phillipe, life did not have any meaning or joy, it lead only to confusion. What he believed to be true *intellectually* contradicted what he felt to be true *experientially*.

The Source of Love

Do you recognize love to be a reality in the world? Theism recognizes love to be real because God is the source of that love. As St. John wrote, "love is from God," and "we love because He first loved us." Atheism, to be logically consistent, must deny the mystery of love; love cannot exist other than as a physical response because there is no infinite being or reality and we are but mere animals.

In recent years, the musical adaptation of Victor Hugo's novel *Les Misérables* took the theater world by storm. When I witnessed this magnificent theatrical production, I was moved to tears. In fact, I doubt there was a dry eye in the audience. When I reflected upon why we, the audience, responded with such emotion, I realized that we were all deeply touched by the depth of love displayed by Jean Valjean, the main character.

Valjean's life was truly the consummate example of sacrificial love. He cared for others, empathized with their hurts, and was willing to lay down his life for those he loved. He was totally selfless, and as he lay dying, the last words he uttered brought the house down:

> Take my love,
> For love is everlasting.
> And remember
> The truth that once was spoken:
> To love another person
> Is to see the face of God.

Christian theism says that love is more than the expression of mere feelings toward someone. It is responding to those we love, not out of selfishness or conceit, but in humility and reverence, placing their well-being above our own. Love is patient and kind, never jealous or envious, never selfish or rude. Love does not demand its own way. It does not hold bitter grudges, for it is characterized by forgiveness. Love accepts the shortcomings of others and seeks to encourage and support them in times of trouble. True love is open and honest, with a willingness to share from the heart. It is not superficial. Love will always believe in the other person, always expect the best of the other person, and always remain steadfast and loyal.

Theism postulates that God designed life to be lived out in relationships characterized by this type of love. The atheist will challenge this position and ask why the world we live in is not characterized by this picture of love. Violence and hatred seem to envelope the world. Murder and assault, divorce and child abuse, bitterness and oppression are commonplace in even the most civilized countries.

The theist will respond, "Perhaps the world is not characterized by love because people leave God—the source of love—out of their lives." As

Alexander Solzhenitsyn lamented in his speech upon receiving the Templeton Award for Religion, the problem with our world is that "Men have forgotten God."

The Great Contradiction of Atheism

The atheist, who believes that religion is an illusion at best and a fraud at worst, should stop and take a long, hard look at the foundations of his intellectual position. After years of reflecting upon the conflicting beliefs of atheism and theism, I have made the decision that a belief in atheism presents an insurmountable contradiction.

Atheism tells me that God is dead, and therefore love is dead, morality is dead, and human life has no value. The contradiction is revealed when the atheist is not able to live a life consistent with the world he professes to believe in. A modern atheistic biology professor, for example, may complain that blacks in South Africa are treated as beasts, but later in biology class, he presents the belief that men are merely sophisticated beasts, the product of an irrefutable evolutionary process. An atheistic political scientist attacks oppressive governments for trampling on the inalienable rights of man, while in the same breath he will deny that there is a moral imperative dictated by a transcendent reality. The atheist allows that natural selection is the supreme law of nature, but then curses the fascist or the tyrant for living by the principles derived from that law.

The twentieth century atheist claims that there is no such thing as love, and yet he loves. He says there is no beauty, yet he continues to be enamored by sunsets. One day he will tell you that because there is no God, there are no absolutes; therefore, justice and cruelty have no meaning. The next evening, while watching the news, he will rail against the unjust and cruel governments of the world.

Dr. Norman Geisler, a highly regarded Christian philosopher, tells the story of a philosophy student in an upper level philosophy course. The student wrote a research paper arguing that there is no God; consequently, he went on to argue, there can be no objective or absolute moral principles. Judged by the paper's research, scholarship, and argumentation, most would have agreed it was easily an *A* paper. The professor, however, wrote these words on the paper: *F—I do not like this blue folder*.

The student stormed into the professor's office waving his paper, protesting, "This is not fair! This is totally unjust! Why should I be graded on the color of the folder. It should have been graded on its contents, not its color!"

Once the student had settled down, the professor asked quietly, "Was this the paper which argued that on the basis of the godless universe in which we live, there are no objective moral principles such as fairness and justice? Did you not also argue that everything is a matter of one's subjective likes and dislikes?"

"Yes . . . yes . . . ," the student replied hesitantly.

"Well then," said the professor, "I do not like blue folders. The grade will remain an *F*."

Abruptly, the face of the young man changed. It struck him that he really did believe in objective moral principles such as fairness and justice. As the professor changed the grade to an *A*, the student left with a new understanding of the objective nature of morality. It is easy to proclaim that there is no God, but it is impossible to live consistently and honestly within the resulting atheistic framework.

Friedrich Nietzsche, the philosopher who coined the phrase "God is dead," clearly recognized the hypocrisy that existed among those who claimed to be atheists. He had great contempt for those who didn't believe in God and yet still clung to a belief in truth, morality, love, and human dignity. To Nietzsche this hypocrisy was as great, if not greater because of its intellectual sloppiness, than the hypocrisy he witnessed within the ranks of organized religion. The behavior of those intellectuals who believed in God was at least coherent and consistent with what they believed. Nietzsche was determined to face the intellectual challenge of living with the consequences of atheism, believing and acting upon the belief in a godless universe.

With great courage, Nietzsche attempted to *practice* atheism until the day he died. As Jean Paul Sartre said, such a life is "a cruel and long-range affair," a life where love, beauty, and meaning could not exist. Nietzsche eventually went insane, suffering from the horrors of syphilis and spending the balance of his rapidly declining life in an asylum.

Dr. Francis Schaeffer, in his book *How Should We Then Live*, states his belief that Nietzsche lost his sanity, in part, because "he understood that insanity was the only philosophic answer if the infinite personal God does not exist." Nietzsche resided from 1881 to 1888 in the beautiful village of Silas Maria in the Swiss Engadine. This brilliant man was surrounded by some of the most beautiful scenery in the world, yet he still faced the tension and despair of atheism. As an intellectual, Nietzsche reasoned that if God is dead, then truth, beauty, and meaning must also be dead; as a human being, he cried out for meaning that can only be found in the existence of the infinite, personal God. Therein lies the great contradiction of atheism. It is an intellectually interesting argument that falls flat when confronted with reality and honesty.

One of the most well known and influential atheists of our time was Jean Paul Sartre, the French novelist, playwright, and leading exponent of Existentialism. His famous works include *Nausea* and *Being and Nothingness*. The message he communicates in all of his work affords an incessant reminder that life and human endeavor is and shall remain useless. Ironically, on his deathbed he lamented, "My atheistic philosophy has failed me; maybe there is a need to believe in a transcendent being and a god."

For years, George Bernard Shaw, the famous British playwright who many consider to be among the most influential figures in modern literature, was an outspoken atheist. However, Shaw reached a point in his life where he confessed a spiritual confusion. "I am an atheist," he admitted, "who has lost his faith."

As Shaw so wryly expressed it, both atheism and theism demand faith— not a naive, shot-in-the-dark type of faith, but rather a faith that the influential German philosopher Schopenhauer has termed a sophisticated one—a faith which after examination and interpretation will inevitably lead you to embrace one of two statements: "I believe God does not exist" or "I believe God does exist." Ultimately, one or the other of these complex but simple statements must be true. Agnosticism—that is, the unwillingness to accept either of these statements—is hardly more than a pedantic term for intellectual sloth. There is either an infinite personal God or there is not. There is no middle ground.

After years as an atheist, C. E. Joad, former head of the philosophy department at the University of London, startled his colleagues one day with the declaration that he had converted to Christianity. He stated that wishful thinking had not lead him to this decision, but intellectual observation and recollection. After years of study, he said, it became apparent to him that the theistic view of life covered more of the facts of experience than any other philosophy, and, therefore, as he put it, "I have been gradually lead to embrace it."

Of the years you have lived, what have you observed and experienced? Have you ever truly loved or been loved? Does human life have an intrinsic value? Have you witnessed the handiwork of the infinite, personal God? If your experience conflicts with your intellectual perspective perhaps it would be wise to re-examine not the experience but rather the intellectual perspective.

Every existing thing is born without reason, prolongs itself out of weakness, and dies by chance.

Jean Paul Sartre

A Purpose In Life

Philosophers who have embraced an atheistic world view implicitly believe we come into this world devoid of any inherent worth, meaning, or direction. Perhaps these philosophers would suggest we sympathize with Shakespeare's Macbeth and not condemn him for his excessive ambitions; after all, perhaps Macbeth was correct when he described life as "a tale told by an idiot, full of sound and fury, signifying nothing."

For the atheist, the heart of reality is darkness and emptiness. Life is nothing more than a chemical accident that resulted when just the right chemicals came together in a primordial soup, in the right place under the right conditions. In fact, the atheist's belief that there is no grand mind who designed our lives must ultimately lead to the conclusion that life has no purpose or meaning—purpose and meaning cannot arise from nothingness.

Everyone, at various stages of their lives, will stop and examine their existence, and ask "Does my life count for anything? Does my life have any meaning or purpose?" We each have a tremendous need to believe that our life is significant and has value.

REMEMBERING THE FORGOTTEN GOD

The Meaningless Existence

The modern playwright, Samuel Beckett, who was not a believer in God, wrote about the power and despair of "nothing" in his most famous work, *Waiting for Godot*. Beckett described humanity's plight as being adrift in nothingness. In the play, he confronts the audience with two questions: What are we doing here? and Are we needed? These are questions that haunted Beckett all his life.

Over the years, I have become a real fan of Woody Allen's films, although I disagree with the spiritual premise of most of his work. Allen's films revel in man's search for meaning and truth. It is clear that Mr. Allen, an atheist (or, as he likes to think of himself, "a hopeful agnostic"), delights in a totally pessimistic view of life, once stating publicly his belief that after the search for truth is concluded man is left with a terrible emptiness:

> "—alienation, loneliness, and emptiness verging on madness. The fundamental things behind all motivation and all activity is the constant struggle against annihilation and against death. It's absolutely stupefying in its terror, and renders anyone's accomplishments meaningless."

Ingmar Bergman, the great Swedish director, exerted a tremendous influence on Allen's work. Bergman, whose films are dark and melancholy, once commented on man's existence: "You were born without purpose. When you die you are extinguished. From being you will be transformed to non-being." Unlike Bergman, however, Woody Allen does not put such a dark face on the world of madness; instead, he makes light of the situation with humor. Experiencing what he declares to be the emptiness of our existence, Allen suggests that life is nothing more than a cruel joke. It is his way of expressing the idea that life is absurd.

In the movie *Play it Again, Sam*, Allen plays the role of a confused divorcé. In his loneliness and insecurity, he desperately attempts to pick up women. At a museum of modern art, he approaches a lovely young woman who is admiring one of Jackson Pollack's paintings of random drippings.

Allen: What do you see in this?

Woman: It reinstates the negativeness of existence. Nothingness. The hideous lonely emptiness of the universe. The predicament of man forced to live in a godless, barren eternity, like a tiny flame flickering in an immense void with nothing but waste, horror, and degradation forming a useless bleak straight jacket in a black absurd cosmos.

Allen: (*Nodding in agreement as he looks at the painting.*) What are you doing Saturday night?

Woman: Committing suicide.

Allen: Well . . .what are you doing Friday night?

This woman's description of the Pollack painting is a true reflection of the nihilism found in modern atheistic philosophy. It leads only to despair, and therefore suicide is indeed a moral solution to be considered. I, too, believe that if life has no meaning, then the short existence we have on this earth will be painfully grim. Instead of having to endure it, why not simply put an end to life?

Thomas Masaryk, the first president of liberated Czechoslovakia after World War I, wrote a book entitled *Suicide and the Meaning of Civilization.* The thesis of the book is that the more godless a society becomes, the higher the rate of suicide. His research suggested that in the Middle Ages, the number of suicides was negligible. However, by the end of the nineteenth century, it was evident that suicide had become one of the top causes of death. Furthermore, Masaryk uncovered the fact that the vast majority of these deaths occurred among highly principled, well-educated people who had no religious faith. His conclusion reveals the tragic story of those individuals who can find no purpose in life and therefore have no reason to live.

It is clear that Woody Allen accepts the position that there can be no meaning in life if there is no God. He further understands that meaninglessness inevitably leads to despair, with suicide as an option. However, in typical fashion, Allen masks the despair of his worldview with humor. Laughter takes the place of despair.

In another of his very popular films, *Hannah and Her Sisters*, Allen plays the role of a hypochondriac who cannot find meaning in life. On one occasion he tries to explain to his mother why he does not believe in God. He asks her, "If there is a God, why were there Nazis?"

His mother looks over to her husband, who is totally disinterested in the conversation. She says to him, "Max, tell your son why God allowed Nazis."

Annoyed by her question, Max responds, "How do I know? I don't even know how the electric can opener works."

Here, Allen makes reference to a question that has plagued theologians and philosophers for centuries. If there is a good God, why does He allow such evil to exist. For Allen there is no answer, so instead of allowing this to breed a mood of pessimism, he again uses humor. For Allen, absurdity and cynicism are much more desirable than the depressing alternative.

In the true story portrayed in the film "Chariots of Fire" we get a glimpse into the life of the great athlete Harold Abrams. Prior to the most significant race of his life—the 100–meter dash for the Olympic gold medal—he looks deep into the eyes of his best friend and says, "I used to be afraid to lose, now I am afraid to win. I have ten seconds to prove the reason for my existence, and even then, I am not sure I will."

Ravi Zacharias, in reference to Abrams' somber statement, observed that even life's pleasures and successes are often accompanied by feelings of pointlessness; they are here for a moment and then gone. At best, pleasure and success have *liftoff* power; sadly, they have no *staying* power to sustain and ultimately fulfill our lives.

When we stop long enough to consider the reason for existence, we are forced to acknowledge that we do not know why we are here. Further reflection could just as easily lead us to the conclusion that life is pointless as it could to the conclusion that life has meaning. However, instead of confronting either prospect, we typically launch into some kind of activity, work or pleasure—anything which will help us postpone having to accept the true condition of our existence. We are as Blaise Pascal has described, "fugitives from reality."

An article in *Time* magazine adequately expressed how the godless world view of the twentieth century culminates in a life of emptiness. In describing this century, the article speaks of a persistent cry of aloneness, a sense that certainty and absolutes are being stripped away, and that each individual is left "isolated with homeless terrors, deterioration, and death." Where painters, poets, composers, and philosophers once held that truth was beauty, they now produce works where truth is "achingly ugly" and beauty is but "a mirage of the memory." Many of the century's most imaginative artists—from Jackson Pollack to Samuel Beckett to Jean Paul Sartre and Albert Camus—poured their lives into the exploration of emptiness and nothingness in a world where God is nothing more than a myth.

The Purposeful Existence

Charles Colson, in his book *Kingdoms In Conflict*, insists that mankind must have purpose and meaning in life in order to exist. He describes a Nazi concentration camp in Hungary, where Jewish prisoners lived under horrible conditions and performed backbreaking work in one of the Nazi's giant factories. As Colson described it:

Then one day Allied aircraft blasted the area and destroyed the hated factory. The next morning several hundred inmates were herded to one end of its charred remains. Expecting orders to begin rebuilding, they were startled when the Nazi officer commanded them to shovel sand into carts and drag it to the other end of the plant.

The next day the process was repeated in reverse; they were ordered to move the huge pile of sand back to the other end of the compound. A mistake has been made, they thought. Stupid swine. Day after day they hauled the same pile of sand from one end of the camp to the other.

Finally, one old man began crying uncontrollably; the guard hauled him away. Another screamed until he was beaten into silence. Then a young man who had survived three years in the camp darted away from the group. The guards shouted for him to stop as he ran toward the electrified fence. The other prisoners cried out, but it was too late; there was a blinding flash and a terrible siz-zling noise as smoke puffed from his smoldering flesh.

In the days that followed, dozens of the prisoners went mad and mean from their work, only to be shot by the guards or electrocuted by the fence. The commandant smugly remarked that there soon would be no more need to use the crematorium.

Human beings need to live purposeful lives. The story that Colson shares suggests that a purposeless life will cause the mind to snap. If God stands behind our existence, and if He placed us here to fulfill a designed purpose, the conclusion Colson comes to should not be surprising. It stands to reason that God, the designer, would provide a purpose that fits the needs of man. The question remains: what is that purpose?

Whenever something is created by a rational mind, isn't it done so for a reason? Would you not agree that the one who chooses to create will also bestow a purpose on the object of his creativity? A chair is created for a reason, therefore a chair has a purpose. A painting is created for a reason, therefore it has a purpose. A fountain pen is designed for a reason, and therefore, it has a purpose. Do you remember the joy of a creative act in your life? Why, do you imagine, would God choose to place human beings on this planet? What could be the reason for this decision?

The Longings of the Heart

In his book *In the Presence of Mine Enemies*, Howard Rutledge, an Air Force pilot who was shot down over North Vietnam and imprisoned, shares an interesting insight he gained while in prison:

> During those longer periods of enforced reflection, it became so much easier to separate the important from the trivial, the worthwhile from the waste. For example, in the past, I usually worked or played hard on Sundays and had no time for church. For years, Phyllis had encouraged me to join the family at church. She never nagged or scolded—she just kept hoping. But I was too busy, too preoccupied, to spend one or two short hours a week thinking about the really important things.
>
> Now the sights and sounds and smells of death were all around me. My hunger for spiritual food soon outdid my hunger for a steak. Now I wanted to know about that part of me that will never die. Now I wanted to talk about God and Christ and the church. But in Heartbreak [the name POWs gave their prison camp] solitary confinement, there was no pastor, no Sunday-school teacher, no Bible, no hymnbook, no community of believers to guide and sustain me. I had completely neglected the spiritual dimension of my life. It took prison to show me how empty life is without God.

Clearly, there can be no grand transcendent purpose for mankind if God is dead. A purposeless life leads only to despair, for life cannot be fulfilling if it is all for nothing. Yet, we all seem to have an innate need for purpose and fulfillment; our hearts long to break from a life that has no meaning. What is it within us that causes our hearts to long for joy, love, and security?

When one examines human motivation, it becomes apparent that we were designed with basic physical needs, such as the need for food, drink, sleep, and sex. And as humans grow and mature into adulthood, we develop more refined needs such as, for example, the need to be clean, to swim in water, to sit in the sun, or to receive a massage. We can categorize these refinements to the basic physical needs as physical desires, i.e., desires for activities and environments which will make us "feel good." Unfortunately, unrestrained physical desire can oftentimes become counter-productive to our best interests; for example, many individuals choose to stimulate their bodies with drugs or alcohol only to eventually experience a decline in physical and mental health and well-being.

In addition to our physical desires, as Mr. Rutledge points out in his prison experience, we also have a spiritual dimension that must be satisfied. We were designed with spiritual desires as well as physical desires. One of Jesus' simplest but most profound statements was to repeat a verse from the Old Testament, "Man does not live by bread alone." He was emphasizing that human life is far more than a physical existence. Not only do we have physical needs to be met, we also have spiritual needs and longings which seek to be fulfilled. We enter this life and search each day thereafter for that which will satisfy both the physical *and* spiritual dimensions of our lives. Only by adequately satisfying these twin desires will a person be whole and complete.

Spiritual desires spring forth from the soul of a person, the soul being comprised of the mind, the will, and the emotions. At a minimum, these spiritual desires can be identified as the longings of the soul.

•The longing for happiness and joy.
•The longing for peace and security.
•The longing to love and be loved.

I recently heard a gentleman speak of a poll he had taken several years ago. In this poll, he interviewed over one thousand high school students, and asked one basic question: "What do you want most out of life?" The top three answers were happiness, love, and peace. It is interesting to note that these students addressed the longings of their souls and not their bodies.

It is obvious that our physical desires must be met in order to sustain life and carry on the human race. Nevertheless, it is the spiritual longing in each of us that drives our lives and motivates us to live as we do. People will spend a lifetime searching for that which they believe will produce happiness, peace, and love, not realizing that what they are actually seeking is to satisfy the spiritual thirst of their souls.

The Great Deception

Few will argue with the proposition that our physical desires and needs can only be satisfied by that which is physical. When we are hungry, we eat food; when we are thirsty, we drink liquids. Applying the same logic, if the spiritual longings of our souls are indeed real and are not physical, they can only be met through a relationship with the source of spirit, the transcendent God.

King David, in one of the Psalms, cries out, "My soul thirsts for God." Every soul has a thirst, a longing that needs to be satisfied. Unfortunately, while everyone may experience this same thirst, many of us refuse to recognize or accept that the thirst is a thirst for God. We deceive ourselves into believing that the physical world and all the things in it are capable of satisfying the yearnings of the heart and the demands of the soul. As the apostle Paul observed, we "have exchanged the truth of God for a lie, and worship and seek after the things in the created world, instead of the Creator Himself."

We all are easily deceived by the notion that if only we had more money, a bigger house, a better job—whatever it is we may believe our lives are lacking—then we will be happy. Take a step back for a moment. Remember the times in your life when you were the most unhappy and unsatisfied. Do Paul's words ring true? Physical pleasure and comfort cannot satisfy our spiritual longings. Does your experience support this truth?

Several years ago, a young, upwardly mobile, New York stockbroker tragically ended his life. He had achieved great wealth, and was soon to marry a beautiful and glamorous young woman. One day, after a setback in the market, he jumped from his high-rise Manhattan apartment to his death. As one journalist summed up the tragedy of the suicide: "He had everything life had to offer, but everything was not enough."

In his book *Mere Christianity*, C. S. Lewis suggests that a false notion has been put into the head of mankind—the idea that men can take the place of God, be their own masters, and in doing so . . .

. . . invent some sort of happiness for themselves outside of God, apart from God. And out of that hopeless attempt has come nearly all that we call human history—greed, poverty, selfish ambition, war, prostitution, classes, brutal empires, slavery— the long terrible story of man trying to find something other than God which will make him happy.

The reason why it can never succeed in this? God made us: invented us as a man invents an engine. A car is made to run on gasoline, and it would not properly on anything else. God designed humans to run on Himself. He Himself is the fuel our spirits were designed to burn, or the food our spirits were designed to feed on. There is no other. That is why it is just no good asking God to make us happy in our own way, without bothering to have a relationship with Himself. God cannot give us a happiness and peace apart from Himself, because it is not there. There is no such thing.

Theism asserts that it is God who stands behind human life, and it is He who placed us here with a purpose in mind for this creation. Furthermore, the Judeo-Christian tradition holds that we think, reason, and communicate because God thinks, reasons, and communicates. The mysterious object of our ability to think, reason, and communicate is God Himself and the act of thinking, reasoning, and communicating becomes the glory of God's creation and the honor of God Himself.

In the first chapter of the Bible, we are told that human beings were "created in the image of God." Obviously, this does not mean we are carbon copies of God. It does mean, however, that God's image is reflected in our capacity to reason and in our ability to love and experience emotion. We each express remarkable and unique personalities and abilities. This human being is mathematic and technical; that one is intuitive and verbal. We are black, we are white; we are male, we are female; we are Irish, we are Chinese. Old, young; rich, poor. In a perfect, Godly society, no one is better than another.

Since it was God who chose to bring forth human existence, it is certain that there must be a reason behind this creation. The God of the Bible is a loving and rational God. Just as parents are motivated to bring children into the world, God brought the human race into being that He might delight in and enjoy a loving relationship with them. The Psalmist declares, "The Lord takes pleasure in His people!"

God created human beings for Himself. "For by Him all things were created, both in the heavens and on earth, visible and invisible, whether thrones or dominions or rulers or authorities, all things have been created by Him and for Him." He designed the human race with the intent that every individual should live out life in a loving relationship with Him. For this reason, life's greatest joy and ultimate satisfaction is experienced only when an individual fulfills the purpose of existence—living in a personal, loving relationship with the Creator.

If this is true, the person who chooses to live a life without God will find that as time passes, despite worldly, material success, life remains incomplete and void of real meaning. Augustine affirmed his belief in this proposition when he said: "God has created us for Himself and our hearts will not find rest until it rests in Him." If we were designed to live in a relationship with God and yet we refuse Him the proper place in our lives, eventually the result will be our malfunctioning as human beings. It is similar to a child *refusing* to love his parents and, by doing so, *choosing* to go through every stage of life without *accepting* their love and emotional support. The parents continue to offer love; the child, however, refuses to accept it. The consequences of such a direction are devastating.

I might add that whenever I speak with someone about this issue of *purpose* and I ask them to consider the fact that God *created* human life, generally I will be questioned about the *process* of man's arrival on earth. Even atheists will agree that it requires a leap of faith to imagine human personality arising from non-living matter. And there are many theists who are evolutionists, believing that God *created* man and established man's *purpose* through the *process* of evolution. At this juncture, all that is important to recognize is that either God initiated the existence of man or he didn't and that either position requires a leap of faith. The theist believes that God stands behind our *creation*, regardless of the *process* by which He may have chosen to bring us here, and that in so doing He has a purpose for each of us.

God's Plan For Us

If each of us is designed by and for God, in His image, with the ability to love, reason, and communicate, then God cannot possibly favor any element of mankind over another. The primary object of our several abilities is to live in a loving relationship with God Himself. He loves us all equally; every human life has untold value and there is no place in a Godly world for discrimination because of race, sex, power, or intelligence.

I run into so many individuals—at all levels of society—whose life experiences have offered nothing but pain, loneliness, and disappointment. Life, they tell me, has not turned out the way they thought it would. In our youths, we envision a perfect life, yet as time passes we encounter the harsh realities of the world. The fantasy, Madison-Avenue life presented on television and in film contributes to the problem, raising our expectations of the wonderful life that awaits us around every corner. When we become aware of the fact that life is difficult and painful, we then become convinced that God has discriminated against us, for He is the one who dealt us such a bad hand.

What many of us fail to recognize is that we live in a world that often deceives us, that leads us away from God's plan. The world attempts to persuade us that in order to have it all, to be truly complete and happy, we must be—

• Wealthy and successful in business
• Attractive and successful with the opposite sex
• Important socially and politically
• Intelligent and well-educated
• Athletic and in good health

We presume, and in many cases accept, that these are the ingredients that make for a happy, fulfilled, and contented life.

So many people, young and old, rich and poor, do not like themselves nor the life they lead. In reality, if we are honest with ourselves, none of us will ever measure up to the illusions of the world's shifting standards. And even if we delude ourselves into believing that we do indeed measure up, that delusion will not last. Consequently, at some point each of us will realize that the world is declaring us to be inadequate creatures, that we are losers. This could help explain why the rate of suicide and mental and emotional breakdown are at an all time high.

But there is good news.

The theist believes that wholeness and completeness in life are the result of a personal relationship with God, who deeply loves each and every one of us, just as we are; we do indeed have the ability to be content with ourselves and our circumstances. We can each know that God has not discriminated against us, for even if we are—

• Poor, middle class, or rich
• Unattractive or attractive, with or without a romantic relationship
• Insignificant in the eyes of others or socially prominent
• Educated or uneducated
• Unathletic or athletic

—we are still loved. Under this timeless and true standard, one may be a failure in the eyes of the world, yet nonetheless experience a full, rich, and satisfying life, living each day in a relationship with God.

The apostle Paul, while sitting in an unclean, foul prison cell penned these amazing and truly remarkable words:

> For I have learned to be content whatever the circumstances. I know what it is to be in need, and I know what it is to have plenty. I have learned the secret of being content in any and every situation, whether well fed or hungry, whether living in plenty or in want.

I will always remember listening to the powerful story of Joni Eareckson Tada, who as a beautiful young woman was forced to face living out her life in a wheelchair because of a diving accident. Looking back to that eventful day she tells us that she would not have traded her wheelchair for anything, for if she had not had this accident, she would never have slowed down long enough to discover the joy of knowing Jesus Christ as her Lord.

This is a staggering statement when one fully considers what this young woman is saying. She is declaring to each of us that the joy and fulfillment that results from a relationship with God is the most significant experience in life. Nothing a person desires can compare with it. She boldly asserts that this relationship is worth losing everything for, whatever is required to humble us and bring us to this wonderful experience, for to know God personally is to fulfill the purpose of existence.

We do not have to wait for devastating circumstances to slow us down or humble us. We have a present opportunity to pursue a personal relationship with God as we recognize it to be the wisest choice in life.

That which has purpose cannot exist by accident. It is purposeful by design, and thus must have a designer behind it. God has designed each one of us to build our lives upon and live them out in a spiritual relationship with Him. It is the greatest of all relationships, one which will result in complete joy and peace. As we center our lives in Him, He gives us a greater ability to enjoy the physical pleasures of the world, and He gives us the wisdom to understand their proper place in our lives.

He, alone, is able to satisfy the thirst of our souls.

My faith is not built on arguments of logic or reason, it is built on revelation.

Fyodor Dostoyevsky

Does God Have A Name?

Over the last few years, I have had a number of opportunities to engage in long, lively discussions with a bright, young architecture graduate student. Perhaps the best way to describe this young man would be to call him a contrarian. Four years ago, he professed to be an atheist and fiercely defended his intellectual position. Two years later, he surprised me when he announced that he was not really sure what he believed. Recently, he has come full circle, acknowledging that there must indeed be a transcendent force in the universe. He had made the choice, he declared: theism—not atheism—was more in line with his actual experience of life.

I was overjoyed to hear of this new spiritual development in my friend's life, and I felt compelled to inquire about his new belief. I asked him to acquaint me with this deity he now believed in. What is this god's name, I asked. What is he or she like? Does this god require anything of us? Is this god involved in the affairs of men?

My friend did not have a response to these questions. Nor, to my surprise, did he seem interested in finding the answers. He seemed to be saying that he was so comfortable with his newfound belief in an infinite presence in the universe that he really didn't want to begin a new struggle with questions to which, in his opinion and in all likelihood, there can be no answers.

Though the evidence may point to the existence of a transcendental, infinite spiritual force in the universe, this force must remain a nameless, unknown deity, unless it appears and reveals its identity. Finite human beings are not capable of knowing or understanding the full essence of the infinite. Therefore, as finite beings, we are forced to acknowledge that any search for God's identity becomes an effort in futility—unless that is, God chooses to reveal himself in a convincing manner.

Anthony Flew, professor of philosophy at York University, has illustrated the idea, in what has become a widely popular parable, that God can never be known. Two men stumble upon a beautiful garden in the midst of a dense forest. The two men logically assume there must be a gardener. They wait for a long time, yet no gardener appears. The first man concludes that no gardener exists even though the flowers are set out in neat, well-kept rows; this garden, he contends, is simply the consequence of an unknown natural process, an aberration in the natural scheme and contrary to the principal of entropy. The second man urges patience, arguing that there has to be a gardener for they both can clearly see that the garden remains orderly.

The gardener must be invisible, the second man surmises. Deciding to test this new premise, they surround the garden with an electric field that will set off an alarm and reveal the presence of this invisible gardener. They wait for quite some time; yet, again, no gardener appears. They now reach the conclusion that even though an orderly garden exists, there is no gardener to be known because one has not appeared. Mr. Flew applies this illustration to our world and states that just as there is no gardener in the story, there must be no God we can know for He has failed to make an appearance.

Ravi Zacharias, who shares Mr. Flew's illustration often in his lectures, puts an altogether different spin on its conclusion. "Mr. Anthony Flew in his story of the garden has in effect nailed the coffin shut on every major religion in the world, except Christianity, for in Christianity, the gardener has appeared in the person of Jesus Christ."

Malcolm Muggeridge, the brilliant British essayist, has noted that plenty of great teachers, mystics, martyrs, and saints have made their appearance at different times in the world, having lived lives and spoken words full of grace and truth for which we have reason to be grateful. Nevertheless, Muggeridge continues, man needs God's special revelation on which he can build a religious belief and from which he can find wisdom and understanding. Muggeridge goes on to say that the only solution is for God to become man, which He did through the Incarnation in the person of Jesus Christ. God thereby "set a window in the dark dungeons of our soul," that He might "let in a light which would provide a view, and offer a way to be released from the misery of our self-centeredness and pride." In Jesus, "eternity steps into time, and time loses itself in eternity."

Several years ago on the Dick Cavett Show, Jane Fonda and the Archbishop of Canterbury appeared as guests. During the course of the show, these two guests had an interesting exchange.

Archbishop: Jesus Christ is the Son of God, you know.

Fonda: Maybe he is for you, but not for me.

Archbishop: Well, either He is or he is not.

The Archbishop's pointed response to Ms. Fonda leads to the next critical question in our search for God. As theists, we recognize that since man is finite and incapable of discovering God on his own ability, God will remain unknown and unknowable unless He reveals or has already revealed Himself. The argument has been made for two thousand years that Jesus Christ is the manifestation of our Creator.

It is a powerful and explosive assertion, an assertion that must be addressed and answered. Either Jesus of Nazareth—a man whose life was documented by historians of the day—is the Son of God, or he is not. Either He spoke the truth about Himself, or he lied. There can be no two ways about it. If He is the Son of God, then we have to decide what we are going to do with Him. If he is not, then our search for God's identity should take an altogether different turn—leading us perhaps to the philosophy of deism, that is, the belief that God exists but cannot be known.

A Man of History

I find it ridiculous as well as sad that certain individuals will attempt to explain away Jesus by asserting that he never existed. With no evidence to support their view, these individuals assert that Jesus is mythological, just like the Greek and Roman gods. No reliable authority on ancient history will support this outlandish contention. They will tell you that Jesus Christ was as real as any other ancient figure of history.

So abundant is the testimony which points to Christ's historical existence that Dr. F. F. Bruce, professor of Biblical criticism at the University of Manchester in England, suggests that reputable historians could not possibly propagate this theory. "Some writers may toy with the fancy of a 'Christ myth,' but they do not do so on the ground of historical evidence. The historicity of Christ is as axiomatic for an unbiased historian as the historicity of Julius Caesar."

The noted scholar J. B. Phillips, after years of historical research, echoes the conviction of Professor Bruce. "I have read in Greek and Latin scores of myths, but I did not find the slightest flavor of myth in the life of Jesus. There is no hysteria, no careful working for effect and no attempt at collusion."

Even the great skeptic and humanist Rousseau claimed "if men could invent such a story and convince others to believe it, they would be greater and more astonishing than Jesus Himself."

The Resurrection

Almost any contemporary Roman history book reveals that not only did Jesus of Nazareth actually exist, but that he was also a great teacher with a tremendous following—a following so strong the influential Roman emperor Constantine would declare Christianity to be the official religion of the entire

Roman empire in 324 AD. The weight of history also does not question the fact that Jesus was crucified by the Roman procurator of Judea, Pontius Pilate. Particularly intriguing is the fact that historians even agree that Jesus was laid in a tomb and, somehow, his body turned up missing three days later. However, an explanation for the missing body is rarely if ever dealt with in any of the modern history textbooks.

The historical sleuth will find it interesting, for example, that H. G. Wells, in *The Outline of History*, accurately describes the life and death of Jesus. However, like so many other historians, he makes no mention of a resurrection, but immediately launches into a description of the explosive growth of the early Christian church and the bold teachings of its disciples. Wells refuses to make a connection between the meteoric rise of the largest institution in the history of the world and the fact that it began in Jerusalem in 33 AD. when the Apostles began to preach that Jesus Christ had risen from the dead. It appears that Wells, along with many other historians, simply does not want to deal with the Apostles' message to the world—Jesus Christ rising from the dead—preferring not to broach the matter at all.

There are times for us all when our faith may be challenged or even ridiculed by another as being "intellectually sloppy." Could it be that those who challenge these precious beliefs are projecting their own fears and anxieties in levelling the challenge, not even affording an opportunity for discussion? After all, what self-respecting intellectual in the modern age would deign to address an issue involving a supernatural event? Isn't it possible that Wells simply omitted this part of Christ's story because of the supernatural aspect of the claim?

In a recent *U. S. News and World Report*, an article gave an extensive and interesting account of the last days of Jesus. I found the article particularly interesting and encouraging in that a prominent, well-respected, *secular* magazine was willing to address the historical accuracy of the resurrection when for most of the twentieth century the subject has been foreclosed. The article stated:

> Yet even the most skeptical Biblical scholars concede that something extraordinary happened in Jerusalem after Good Friday to account for the radical change in the behavior of the disciples, who at Jesus' arrest had fled to their own homes in fear. Could Jesus' resurrection account for the fact that within a few weeks they were boldly preaching their message to the very people who sought to crush them?

John Locke, the gifted eighteenth century English philosopher, had much to say concerning the resurrection of Christ. He reasoned that for Christ to be the Messiah, the resurrection must have been a reality—these two articles of Christian faith, the Resurrection and the divinity of Christ, are in reality one and the same. "Our Savior's Resurrection . . . is truly of great importance in Christianity; so great that His being or not being the Messiah stands or falls with it; so that these two important articles are inseparable and in effect make one. For since that time, believe one and you believe both; deny one of them, and you can believe neither."

In the 1950s, a young scholar by the name of Josh McDowell set out to prove through historical inquiry that Jesus did not rise from the dead as Christians over the centuries had proclaimed. He was certain that if he could effectively challenge and cast sufficient doubt on this event, the institutions of Christianity would be in trouble. He correctly reasoned that Jesus' resurrection was the foundational belief which held Christianity together. McDowell recognized, as did the apostle Paul, that if Jesus did not rise from the dead, Christians are hardly more than fools to be pitied.

After years of study, Mr. McDowell astonished his colleagues by declaring that Jesus indeed had risen from the dead. The evidence he discovered during his years of study are documented in the two lengthy volumes *Evidence That Demands a Verdict* and *More Evidence*. Josh McDowell consequently made the decision to convert to Christianity.

Any modern traveler to the city of Jerusalem will attest to the fact that there is no sacred place to visit the entombed body of Jesus Christ. No such place exists because it is a historical fact that the body did indeed disappear. For this reason, countless archaeologists and historians have tried over the years to come up with some type of explanation other than the explanation offered by the Bible that Jesus Christ was resurrected from the dead.

The Missing Body Of Jesus Of Nazareth

Because of the significant ramifications in the choice between the truth and the falsehood of the Biblical account of the Resurrection of Christ, skeptics over the centuries have sought to undermine the Resurrection by attempting to establish alternative explanations for Christ's missing body. These skeptics have advanced two plausible explanations: 1) Roman officials seized the body, or 2) the Disciples stole the body.

As to the first contention that Roman officials seized the body, it indeed would not have been unusual for them to seize and impound the dead body of Jesus, especially since Jesus had publicly (although in somewhat veiled terms) declared that He would rise from the dead. However, there exists one glaring deficiency in this argument. Within days after the death of Jesus, the disciples were boldly proclaiming the bodily resurrection of Jesus based upon His repeated, physical appearance before them. Throughout the streets of Jerusalem multitudes of eager listeners gathered around to hear the tale. There were also an additional five hundred citizens who were ready to corroborate this startling claim for they, too, had seen the resurrected Jesus. The Jewish or Roman authorities had but one very simple thing to do to quash this wild rumor: produce the dead body of Jesus. *Had this been done, Christianity would have died on the spot.* It is obvious they must not have had His body for Christianity is alive and well in the modern world.

The only other feasible explanation that the skeptics have been able to offer—that the disciples must have stolen the body—also has a gaping hole in it. When Jesus was apprehended by the Romans, the disciples fled for their lives in fear. In order to have stolen the body, they would have had to have regained their courage, done battle with the Roman soldiers guarding the grave, retrieved the body, somehow disposed of it without anyone discovering their plot, fabricated the story of his resurrection, and then be convincing enough to proclaim it as truth so that it would have power to influence succeeding generations . . . as indeed it has.

What is by far the most problematic point in this position is why these men would go to their deaths as martyrs preaching with passion a message they *knew* to be false. As Dr. Peter Moore of the Little Trinity Episcopal Church in Toronto, Canada, asks, "Does it seem logical that these men would go through the rest of their lives tenaciously preaching in public that Jesus was alive when they knew all along that his body was decomposing in a Christian hideaway somewhere?" J. N. D. Anderson, director of the Institute of Advanced Legal Studies at the University of London, points out that the theory of the disciples disposing of the body "would run contrary to all we know of them: their ethical teaching, the quality of their lives, their steadfastness in suffering and persecution."

Charles Colson, in his book *Loving God*, delivers a powerful, modern twist to the argument supporting the truth of the Resurrection. He presents his case by analogizing to his own experience in the Watergate cover-up.

> So what does all this have to do with the resurrection of Jesus Christ? Simply this: . . . if one is to assail the historicity of the Resurrection and therefore the deity of Christ, one must conclude that there was a conspiracy—a cover-up, if you will—by eleven men with the complicity of up to five hundred others. To subscribe to this argument, one must also be ready to believe that each disciple was willing to be ostracized by friends and family, live in daily fear of death, endure prisons, live penniless and hungry, sacrifice family, be tortured without mercy, and ultimately die—all without ever once renouncing that Jesus had risen from the dead.
>
> This is why the Watergate experience is so instructive for me. If

John Dean and the rest of us were so panic-stricken, not by the prospect of beatings and execution, but by political disgrace and a possible prison term, one can only speculate about the emotions of the disciples. Unlike the men in the White House, the disciples were powerless people, abandoned by their leader, homeless in a conquered land. Yet they clung tenaciously to their enormously offensive story that their leader had risen from his ignoble death and was alive—and was *the* Lord.

The Watergate cover-up reveals, I think, the true nature of humanity. None of the memoirs suggest that anyone went to the prosecutor's office out of such noble notions as putting the Constitution above the President, or bringing rascals to justice, or even moral indignation. Instead, the writings of those involved are consistent recitations of the frailty of man. Even political zealots at the pinnacle of power will save their own necks in the crunch, though it may be at the expense of the one they profess to serve so zealously.

Is it really likely, then, that a cover-up, a plot to perpetuate a lie about the Resurrection, could have survived the violent persecution of the apostles, the scrutiny of early church councils, the horrendous purge of the first-century believers who were cast by the thousands to the lions for refusing to renounce the Lordship of Christ? Is it not probable that at least one of the apostles would have renounced Christ before being beheaded or stoned? Is it not likely that some "smoking gun" document might have been produced exposing the "Passover plot"? Surely one of the conspirators would have made a deal with the authorities (government and Sanhedrin probably would have welcomed such a soul with open arms and pocketbooks!).

Blaise Pascal, the extraordinary mathematician, scientist, inventor, and logician of the seventeenth century, was convinced of the truth of Christ by examination of the historical record. In his classic *Pensées*, Pascal wrote: "The hypothesis that the apostles were knaves is quite absurd. Follow it out to the end and imagine these twelve [sic] men meeting after Jesus' death and conspiring to say that he had risen from the dead. This means attacking all the powers that be. *The human heart is singularly susceptible to fickleness, to change, to promises, to bribery.* One of them had only to deny his story under these inducements, or still more because of possible imprisonment, torture and death, and they would all have been lost." As Pascal correctly observes, man in his normal state will renounce his beliefs just as readily as Peter renounced Jesus *before* the Resurrection. But as the same Peter discovered *after* the Resurrection, there is a power beyond man that causes him to forsake all. It is the power of the God who revealed Himself in the person of Jesus Christ.

The Reality of the Resurrection

Thus, Christianity stands or falls on the basis of the Resurrection. Many have tried to undermine the historical reliability of this most significant event and have failed. The evidence for the resurrection of Jesus Christ has been examined perhaps as extensively and exhaustively as any other fact in history. The great legal scholar Simon Greenleaf, a prominent professor of law at Harvard for fifteen years, was asked to examine the historical evidence for the Resurrection and apply the laws of evidence to it. After concluding his study, Greenleaf was convinced that the Resurrection was an historical event that could be proven true beyond a reasonable doubt based on the historical evidence.

In the resulting work, *An Examination of the Testimony of The Four Evangelists by the Rules of Evidence Administered in the Courts of Justice*, Greenleaf seized on the fact that the apostles resolutely declared that Christ had risen from the dead. They asserted this doctrine with a unified voice, in the face of great discouragement. Jesus, their master, had recently been executed by crucifixion, the sentence delivered by a public tribunal. The powerful Roman leaders saw the Christian religion as a severe threat to their political power; the apostles and their nascent movement could potentially undermine the very foundations of the *pax Romana* (the Roman imperialist philosophy of governing the empire through "the Roman peace"—allowing local rule and provincial integrity while at the same time keeping an army garrisoned in the vicinity to safeguard obedience). As Greenleaf argues:

> The world was against them. They could expect nothing but contempt, opposition, revilings, bitter persecutions, stripes, imprisonments, torments, and cruel deaths. Yet, this faith they zealously did propagate and all these miseries they endured undismayed, nay, rejoicing. As one after another was put to a miserable death, the survivors only prosecuted their work with increased vigor and resolution. The annals of military warfare afford scarcely an example of the like heroic constancy, patience, and unbending courage. They had every possible motive to review carefully the grounds of their faith, and the evidences of the great fact and truths which they asserted; and these motives were pressed upon their attention with the most melancholy and terrific frequency. It was therefore impossible that they could have persisted in affirming the truths they have narrated, had not Jesus actually risen from the dead, and had they not known this fact as certainly as they knew any other fact.

Thomas Arnold, Regius professor of modern history at Rugby public school in the mid-1800s and author of the distinguished, three-volume work *History of Rome*, wrote:

> I have been used for many years to study the histories of other times, and to examine and weigh the evidence of those who have written about them, and I know of no one fact in the history of mankind which is proved by better and fuller evidence of every sort, to the understanding of a fair inquirer, than the great sign which God hath given us that Christ died and rose again from the dead.

One of the more colorful apologists who has written on this issue is Frank Morison, a brilliant practicing lawyer. Morison describes his perspective as that of a skeptic, "having been brought up in a rationalistic environment," and that because of his background he "had come to the opinion that the resurrection was nothing but a fairy tale happy ending which spoiled the matchless story of Jesus." Morison therefore planned to write a book on the last days of Jesus, outlining the historical event as it actually happened, but with the intention of omitting the supernatural and the miraculous (including the Resurrection) in which he did not believe. However, after careful examination of the historical record, he radically changed his view and concluded his research with his important work *Who Moved the Stone?* The first chapter of this book is appropriately titled "The Book that Refused to be Written." He outlines the overwhelming evidence that points to the veracity and trustworthiness of the history supporting the Resurrection. He, too, focuses on the courage and actions of the apostles in the face of brutal retaliations.

Implications of The Resurrection

How is it that we remember Jesus of Nazareth after these many years? If Jesus Christ truly rose from the dead, as the Bible says, what are the implications of that truth? If Jesus was who He said He was, the Son of God, doesn't this have tremendous ramifications for the community of man? For the modern view of life, death, and the afterlife?

From an objective viewpoint, the life of Christ is a paradox. How could this man named Jesus have made such an impact on civilization, especially given the circumstances in which He lived? As an exercise in reasoning, were you God and had you decided to send your son into the world over two thousand years ago, isn't it likely you would have chosen a different plan altogether, especially if you intended for Him to affect and influence the world for an eternity?

You would in all likelihood have had Jesus born into a wealthy, influential, Roman household, for Rome was where all the power was concentrated. In Rome, he could receive the necessary education and refinement. You would also have placed him in a favorable social position, where he would gain exposure to influence and power. He would need to know the right people. Finally, you would have given him the looks and presence to draw a large number of people to hear his message.

Because God's vision is all-encompassing, His intentions pure, and His wisdom infinite, He often moves and acts in a manner seemingly contrary to human reason. Contrary to our reasonable speculations on how we might have gone about introducing Jesus into the world, God sent Him into a family of humble means. Consequently, Jesus received no formal education and lived His young adult life as a simple carpenter. He spent His entire life in an area called Palestine, which was considered among the most desolate and undesirable regions in the entire Roman Empire.

Jesus clearly never distinguished Himself by accomplishing any of those things which we traditionally associate with historical greatness.

•He never occupied a formal position of power.
•He never commanded an army.
•He had no wealth.
•He had no prominent person to promote His cause.

Yet, His life is considered throughout the western world to be the greatest in all of human history. A mere sampling from the works of respected authors and scholars presses home the degree to which the life of Jesus of Nazareth has influenced our culture. Indeed, the profundity of the life and death of Jesus Christ rests at the very foundations of the modern world.

George Gordon, Lord Byron

Even the great English Romantic poet, Byron, whose verse was widely condemned on moral grounds and whose personal behavior was roundly criticized for its debauchery, was compelled to admit, "If ever man was God or God man, Jesus Christ was both."

Charles Dickens

As Dickens, the great Victorian novelist and social commentarian, author of many classics of English literature including *A Tale of Two Cities*, *Oliver Twist*, and *Great Expectations*, was to write in his later years, "I commit my soul to the mercy of God, through our

Lord and Saviour Jesus Christ. I now most solemnly impress upon
you the truth and beauty of the Christian religion as it came from
Christ himself."

Bernard Ramm

The historian Bernard Ramm said, "Jesus Christ as the God-man is
the greatest personality that ever lived, and therefore His personal
impact is the greatest of any man that ever lived."

Herbert George Wells

When the English novelist H. G. Wells, whose literary output was
vast, extremely varied, often dark and depressing, was asked which
person has had the most significant impact on history, he replied
that "judging a person's greatness by historical standards, Jesus
stands first."

Will Durant

Philosopher Will Durant has said that "in all of Western civilization,
the person who stands out alone among all others is Christ. He
undoubtedly was the most prominent influence on our thoughts."

Clive Staples Lewis

C. S. Lewis, the great English scholar and professor of Medieval
and Renaissance English at Cambridge University, wrote, "I am trying here to prevent anyone saying the really foolish thing that people
often say about Him: 'I am ready to accept Jesus as a great moral
teacher, but I don't accept His claim to be God.' That is the one
thing we must not say. A man who was merely a man and said the
sort of things Jesus said would not be a great moral teacher. He
would either be a lunatic—on a level with the man who says he is a
poached egg—or else he would be the devil of Hell. You must make
your choice. Either this man was, and is, the Son of God: or else a
madman or something worse. You can shut Him up for a fool; you
can spit at Him and kill Him as a demon; or you can fall at His feet

and call Him Lord and God. But let us not come up with any patron-
izing nonsense about His being a great human teacher. He has not
left that open to us. He did not intend to."

William Lecky

William Lecky, one of Great Britain's more noted historians, posit-
ed, "It was reserved for Christianity to present to the world an ideal
character which through all the changes of eighteen centuries has
inspired the hearts of men with an impassioned love; has shown
itself capable of acting on all ages, nations, temperaments, and conditions; has been not only the highest pattern of virtue, but the
strongest incentive to its practice . . . . The simple record of these
three short years of active life has done more to regenerate and soft-
en mankind than all the disquisitions of philosophers and all the
exhortations of moralists."

James Stewart

James Stewart, a Scottish philosopher and minister, wrote, "When I
speak of the mystery of personality in Christ, I am thinking of the
startling coalescence of contrariety that you find in Jesus. He was
the meekest and lowliest of all the sons of men, yet He said that he
would come on the clouds of heaven in the glory of God. He was so
austere that evil spirits and demons cried out in terror at His coming,
yet he was so genial, winsome, and approachable that children loved
to play with Him, and the little ones nestled in His arms. No one
was ever half so kind or compassionate towards sinners, yet no one
ever spoke such red hot scorching words about sin. He would not
break the bruised reed and His whole life was love, yet on one occasion He demanded of the Pharisees how they expected to escape the
damnation of hell. He was a dreamer of dreams and a seer of visions
yet for sheer stark naked realism He has all of our self-styled realists
beaten. He was a servant of all, washing the disciples' feet, yet mas-
terfully he strode into the Temple, and the hucksters and traders fell
over one another in their mad rush to get away from the fire they

saw blazing in His eyes. There is nothing in history to compare with the life of Christ."

Johann Wolfgang von Goethe

The important philosopher and poet Goethe, at the end of his life, as he looked back over the vast field of history, was constrained to confess that "if ever the Divine appeared on earth, it was in the person of Christ; the human mind no matter how far it may advance in every other department, will never transcend the height and moral culture of Christianity as it shines and glows in the gospels."

Phillip Schaff

The historian Phillip Schaff observed that, "[T]his Jesus of Nazareth, without money and arms, conquered more millions than Alexander, Caesar, Mohammed, and Napoleon; without science and learning, He shed more light on things human and divine than all philosophers and scholars combined; without the eloquence of schools, He spoke such words of life as were never spoken before or since and produced effects which lie beyond the reach of orator or poet; without writing a single line, He set more pens in motion and furnished themes for more sermons, orations, discussions, learned volumes, works of art, and songs of praise, than the whole army of great men of ancient and modern times."

Mortimer Adler

Mortimer Adler has written more than twenty-five books, but is perhaps best known for his editorship of the Harvard Great Book series featuring the classics of Western culture. For years an outspoken atheist, Adler has recently been attracted to Christianity. He contends "that Christianity is the only world religion that is evangelical in the sense of sharing good news." The mysteries of life are too incomprehensible and there would be no point of God's revelation "if we could figure it out ourselves."

Malcolm Muggeridge

As he remembers the world events that have taken place over the many years of his life as a writer and essayist, Malcolm Muggeridge observed shortly before his death, "We look back upon history and what do we see, empires rising and falling, revolutions and counter-revolutions, wealth accumulated and wealth dispersed. I look back upon my own fellow countrymen of England who once dominated a quarter of the world, most of them convinced 'the God who made the mighty will make them mightier.' I have heard a crazed cracked German acclaim to the world that he would usher in the world of the German Reich, and that he would be more powerful than any other ruler before him. I have seen an Italian clown with his own arrogant assumption of power. I've seen a murderous Russian in the Kremlin proclaimed to be the wisest and greatest leader to ever live. I have seen America wealthier and more powerful militarily than the rest of the world put together. Had the American people desired, they could have outdone a Caesar or an Alexander in the range and scale of their conquests. I have seen this all in one lifetime, and now gone, gone with the wind. England now threatened with dismemberment and bankruptcy, Hitler and Mussolini dead, remembered only in infamy. Stalin now a forbidden name in the regime he helped found and dominate for some three decades. America is now haunted by the fears of running out of the precious fluid that runs her automobiles, with the horrible memories of a disastrous campaign in Vietnam and the victories of the Don Quixotes of the media as they charged the windmills of Watergate—all in one lifetime—and now gone with the wind."

"Behind the debris of these civilizations," Muggeridge concludes, "stands the gigantic figure of Jesus Christ, because of whom, in whom, and through whom man can ultimately find the answer for himself and for history."

Man is not at peace with his fellow man because he is not at peace with himself; he is not at peace with himself because he is not at peace with God.

Thomas Merton

The Condition of Man

On a network news broadcast, David Brinkley notes with distress that a war is being fought in the streets of America. The war he is speaking of involves savage murders, senseless drive-by shootings, and violent deaths resulting from such trivialities as, for example, a squabble over a pack of cigarettes or a pair of namebrand tennis shoes. Mr. Brinkley goes on to reflect that this runaway crime, this urban street fighting must be the result of a sea change in morals. "Life doesn't mean anything," he remarks, shaking his head. "Human life is no longer valued."

Another major news documentarian, Barbara Walters, asks her viewers what they think is wrong with young people today. A great number of responses reveal that the root of the problem may be a crisis of character. Walters concludes, "Today's high school seniors live in a world of misplaced values. They have no sense of discipline, no goals. They care only for themselves. In short, they are becoming a generation of undisciplined cultural barbarians."

NBC news anchor Tom Brokaw, hosting a special four-hour program on street gangs and the drug problem, spends a considerable amount of time probing the reasons for the violence and the fear, the drug abuse and the poor quality of life in the inner city. It is a very honest and moving presentation. During an interview with an elderly man who has lived for many years in the Watts district of Los Angeles, Brokaw asks, "How could these kids in these gangs lose their values and morals so completely?" How could the morals and values of so many of our nation's teenagers—in the urban ghetto as well as in the wealthy suburb—deteriorate to the point where they would choose to live like animals in a jungle?

• • • •

The above commentaries of Mr. Brokaw, Mr. Brinkley, and Ms. Walters were all made prior to 1992. Each, however, seems to have foreshadowed what eventually took place in the streets of Los Angeles when widespread violence erupted in all corners of the city following the verdict in the Rodney King trial in the spring of that year.

There are those who maintain that the rioting, looting, and burning were honest reactions to the unjust and racist decision rendered in the trial. However, the Reverend E. V. Hill, a black minister in south central Los Angeles, remarked that in his opinion much of the anarchic street activity was merely an opportunity for hoodlums and gangsters "to fill their pantries and living rooms and to replace old furniture."

How should we respond to the senseless and merciless beating of Rodney King as well as the retaliatory beatings of the many other citizens who were merely in the wrong place at the wrong time during the riots which ensued? What has gone wrong with our society?

Charles Colson echoes this concern in his book *Against the Night*:

A *Time* magazine cover story on ethics lamented "What's wrong? Hypocrisy, betrayal, and greed unsettle a nation's soul." While the *Washington Post* wrote of "a society increasingly confronted by incidents in which the actions of adults and children seem bereft of morality and conscience."

"Some experts say the depth of the problem has reached a point where common decency can no longer be described as common," continued the *Post*. Somewhere, somehow, they contend, the traditional value system got disconnected for a growing number of America's next generation. *The New Republic*, identifying the widespread "sense that nothing is prohibited," accuses society of a failure "to teach civilization."

When *The New Republic*, the *Washington Post* and *Time*—none of which are generally recognized as champions of conservative morality—suddenly become concerned with a decline of virtue, some line has surely been crossed.

Even though we live in a world that is depraved and full of evil, we in the western world generally choose to ignore the cultural and social problems that surround us, blocking from our minds the terrifying futures our children can expect. As Carl Henry, educator and author, has put it, "we sit glued to the television set, unmindful that ancient pagan rulers staged colosseum circuses to switch the minds of the restless ones from the realities of a spiritually vagrant empire to the illusion that all is basically well." Unfortunately, only a handful of concerned citizens will stop long enough to carefully examine what is happening to our society.

The Great Debate

One of the classic philosophical debates concerns the issue of man's basic nature. Is man basically good or evil? Is society capable of improving itself through human institutions such as scientific and governmental programs? Secular humanists will argue that recent advances in technology and science have greatly improved the quality of life in relation to that of past generations. A basic tenet of this position is that human intelligence together with enlightened social engineering is capable of creating a better society.

Conditions of poverty, crime, and other grave societal ills will inevitably improve as education spreads throughout a much larger cross-section of society. Any challenge to this humanistic belief is regarded as reactionary and unenlightened thinking.

The Judeo-Christian concept of history holds that society, reflected in human nature, was, is, and shall remain imperfect and flawed. There was never a Golden Age of morality in western culture or indeed in any culture at any time in history. There never has been and never will be a time when all elements of society and culture can be engineered by human knowledge or human effort to work in complete, utopian harmony. The root of the word *utopia*, coined by Sir Thomas More in the sixteenth century, stems, after all, from the Greek for *no place*.

The Christian believes the purpose of life is to live simply and lovingly in an individual relationship with God; to live life, as Jesus commanded, loving God first and foremost and loving one's neighbor as oneself. To the theist, the degree and variety of social ills present today demonstrate a decline in the Godliness of our culture.

Based on your life experience, do you think human beings are naturally evil or naturally good? Many people naively and optimistically respond that man is basically good; yet, doesn't history clearly reveal that although man recognizes and appreciates goodness, he displays the natural tendency to gravitate towards evil and extreme selfishness? How do you honestly assess your life; haven't you, in truth, had to resist a life of self-centeredness?

In Plato's *Republic*, the great Greek philosopher tells the story of a shepherd who watches over the flock of the king. One day, after a mighty storm, there appears a fissure in the ground where his flock is feeding. Astonished by the sight, he goes down into the chasm and discovers a body completely naked except for a marvelous gold ring; he removes the ring and places it on his finger and makes his way out of the crevasse. When he gathers later with the other shepherds, he happens to turn the collet of the ring toward his palm. At once he becomes invisible, and the other shepherds begin to speak of him as if he were not there. When he turns the collet back, he becomes visible again. After discovering this splendid power, he makes his way to the court where he seduces the Queen, and with her help murders the King and seizes the throne.

Plato used this illustration to demonstrate that men do right only under compulsion or by convention. Left on their own they will wrong their neighbor, take their neighbor's belongings, and gravitate towards a life of evil. Plato wrote his *Republic* in 368 BC; it is amazing how consistent mankind has remained throughout the centuries.

Leonardo da Vinci lived most of his life optimistically believing in the nobility of every man. He was convinced that man on his own terms, given his native ability, could solve every problem it faced and ultimately was capable of bringing forth an ideal community. He had complete faith in the ability of man to achieve harmony. However, as time slipped by, Leonardo finally recognized that there was a division between his theory and the way people actually lived their lives. When Francis I, King of France, brought him to the French court, Leonardo was despondent. He lived out the last years of his life completely dejected over the condition of man and the hopelessness of the future of mankind.

The English historian Arnold Toynbee, in his book *Experiences*, relates the story of his family's beliefs and expectations at the turn of the twentieth century. He had a brilliant uncle, who as a scientist and a recognized genius in his field was wildly optimistic about the future. This uncle was convinced that a golden utopian age would soon be ushered in by the advances of science. On the other hand, Toynbee's father, a social worker, was quietly and soberly restrained in his optimism on the future of mankind. At the time, the young, impressionable Toynbee became engaged in his uncle's optimistic outlook, and found his father to be too somber and pessimistic. However, after many years of study and experience, Toynbee concluded that his uncle had in fact been naive and that his father's assessment was absolutely correct. H. G. Wells was another twentieth century thinker who as a young intellectual believed in the perfectibility of man and society. In 1920, he published an extraordinarily ambitious work, *Outline of History*, which also served as his unabashed declaration of idealism. Each page conveyed an unshakeable faith in progress and a conviction of complete optimism for the future. However, a mere thirteen years later, in his book *The Shape of Things to Come*, Wells had clearly shifted perspectives; now, his writing, rather than being optimistic, related the stubbornness and selfishness of people and governments. So radically altered was his consciousness that he even went so far as to maintain that the only solution for mankind was for the intellectual elite (which included himself, of course) to take control of the entire world, forcibly changing people's lives through compulsory education. Twelve years later, in 1945, just shortly before his death, he completed his final work, *The Mind at the End of Its Tether*. In it, he concluded that "there is no way out, or around, or through the impasse . . . ," there is no hope for mankind.

Isn't it true that human depravity has been empirically verified over time? Is it possible that mankind, in all of its creative brilliance, cannot produce a good and perfect society because human beings are naturally self-centered and inevitably gravitate towards a life of evil?

Several years ago, in a segment of *60 Minutes*, Mike Wallace documented the story of the Nazi Adolph Eichmann. Eichmann, who had escaped postwar justice by fleeing Germany and remaining fugitive for over fifteen years, was finally captured and put on trial in the early 1960s. Wallace asked his viewers, "How is it possible for a man to act as Eichmann acted? Was he a monster? A madman? Or was he perhaps something even more terrifying: Was he normal?"

Wallace followed this question with an interview of Yehiel Dinur, a concentration camp survivor who had testified against Eichmann at Eichmann's

1961 trial. A film clip showed Dinur walking into the courtroom. He began to weep uncontrollably and then collapsed on the floor. Dinur explained to Wallace, "I was afraid about myself; I saw that I am capable of doing this. I am exactly like he." Eichmann was no longer that powerful Nazi who had orchestrated the Holocaust, but rather simply an ordinary man.

As Wallace closed the segment he concluded, "Eichmann is in all of us."

In the summer of 1969, four hundred thousand young people spent four days together in upstate New York listening to rock and roll music, getting high, and sleeping together under the stars. There was no violence, no unrest, and as most participants will tell you, the event was surrounded with "complete harmony." At the concert's conclusion, those who had attended adjudged Woodstock to be the beginning of a new and wonderful age. It was "the dawning of the Age of Aquarius." One of the organizers breathlessly proclaimed, "This is the beginning of a new era. It works." An entire generation naively but firmly believed that free love, peace, and drugs would be the vehicles to usher in this new age.

Shortly after Woodstock, the rock heroes Jimi Hendrix and Janice Joplin died of drug overdoses. At Altamont, California, the Rolling Stones headlined a second major rock festival and brought in the Hell's Angels to control the concert. Violence erupted and a man was killed. In the next issue of *Rolling Stone* magazine it was noted that "Our age of innocence is gone." The new era that Woodstock had spawned died a premature and ugly death.

During this same time, Dionne Warwick recorded a hit song, *What the World Needs Now is Love*. It has remained enormously popular over the years, not only because of the quality of the music and the talent of the artist, but because the lyrics communicate a message that all people can relate to. We live in a world of overwhelming anger, where people and cultures commit atrocities against one another. No one with any degree of civility would disagree with the assertion that hatred, jealousy, and bitterness need to be replaced with love. Unfortunately, it did not happen then and it has not happened yet.

REMEMBERING THE FORGOTTEN GOD

Did you know that over two hundred thousand teenagers in the United States attempt suicide each year and that between 1950 and 1977 the suicide rate among teenagers quadrupled for males and doubled for females? Why is it not surprising that while nations threaten each other with atomic destruction, violence darkens our inner cities, and throughout the world, people live in fear and in hunger? We are faced with the problems of AIDS, poverty, divorce, pornography, homelessness, racism, alcoholism, greed, terrorism— the list could go on and on.

As we approach a new century, the scramble is on for solutions to the world's economic and social ills. In this effort, we continue to cling to the institutions we believe are responsible for taking care of us: schools and government. Though I would be the first to acknowledge that these are both vital institutions in any culture, the question remains, can they deliver us from our difficulties? Can they quench our thirsts? Are they our saviors?

The Disparity Between Educational Opportunity and Its Results

Young people spend a large portion of their years in the classroom where they are exposed to the best that modern education can provide. Most educators will agree that while much can be improved, the facilities, resources, and teaching techniques have never been better. It would seem logical that education should provide an appropriate solution to the world's problems. However, one must also ask why are the most educated nations of the world among the most violent? The United States in fact ranks in the highest category for per capita incidence of violent crime. How is it that one of the most civilized and prosperous countries in the world is also one of the most uncivilized in its behavior? Maybe education alone is not the solution.

Since education exerts such a powerful influence on our children, shouldn't we demand to know the degree and kind of influence it is having? Most parents probably have no idea about what, if any, values their children are taught in school; they innocently assume those values must be good and proper. However, though students learn how to read, write, add, and subtract, parents also need to be asking how education is affecting their children's moral behavior.

It seems that modern education in order to avoid controversy—and litigation—seeks to maintain a position of moral neutrality. So as not to offend anyone educators leave the responsibility of value judgements and moral behavior to parents and religious institutions. However, much of the classroom curriculum focuses on issues that inevitably will affect a student's view of life. Therefore, in an attempt to remain morally neutral, the elementary and secondary educational institutions unwittingly become forums where the average student will learn that there is no such thing as absolute right and wrong behavior. In not taking a position, the school is, in effect, saying there are many alternatives to choose from and the student should be tolerant and respectful of *all* alternatives.

Should students tolerate drug abuse? Should they tolerate reckless sexual promiscuity? Should a student be taught to tolerate everything in life, or is there a point where lines must be drawn and value judgements made?

In a free society, there is a critically important place for tolerance. Tolerance of new ideas, tolerance of old ones. Tolerance of those who look different from the majority, tolerance of those who hold different beliefs from the majority. However, there comes a point where tolerance leads to chaos and destruction. In *The Closing of the American Mind*, Allen Bloom calls this new tolerance "the virtue, the only virtue, which all primary education for more than fifty years has dedicated itself to inculcating."

Bloom contends that relativism in education is the dominant force on college campuses today and that it has produced ethical confusion and has corrupted the mind of the university student. Colleges seem to be teaching that the only highly respected virtue in education today is openness. The successful and intellectually superior student must be open to all moral options.

These issues are not confined to the campuses of higher education, however; they can also be found in elementary and secondary institutions as well. I was astounded to read about a high school class in Teaneck, New Jersey, where fifteen students were asked their opinions on the conduct of a young woman who had found one thousand dollars and had turned it in to the local authorities. The students all agreed that she was a fool to turn it in. *The New York Times* reporter who sat in on this class was not only stunned by the students' response, he could not believe that the teacher did not challenge their judgment. After class, the reporter approached the teacher and asked why he had not offered a dissenting opinion. The teacher replied, "If I come from a position that is 'right' and 'wrong,' then I'm not their counselor."

Charles Colson says that every area of education has been infected by this morally neutral philosophy. Colson suggests that there is a tragic irony in this pedagogical position: at one time the pursuit of virtue was not only a specific goal of the classroom, it was the only goal. As Plato said of education, "If you ask what is the good of education, the answer is easy—that education makes good men, and that good men act nobly."

Dr. Carl Henry describes how conspicuous the mandate of moral openness and tolerance is on the college campus as evidenced by the reception President Frank Rhodes of Cornell University received upon addressing a large group of faculty and students at Harvard in 1987. At the podium, Dr. Rhodes suggested that the nation's academic centers need seriously to attend to the "intellectual and moral well-being" of students. During the course of his address, he was frequently interrupted by catcalls from both the students and the faculty. One of the hecklers was even greeted with enthusiastic applause when he asked Dr. Rhodes *who* would provide the moral instruction and *whose* morality would be promoted.

It is obvious that proper education can positively impact adolescents and teenagers when it seeks to "make good men and women" who can distinguish between right and wrong. However, in order to have a set of absolute values which define right and wrong there must be a transcendent source which has revealed these absolute values. While the modern educator will tell you that tolerance in values is a multicultural imperative, the Judeo-Christian community holds that the concepts of right and wrong are specifically defined within the Biblical context. However, in the current environment, American public education has virtually eliminated religious language from the curriculum to the point that teachers cannot even post the Ten Commandments in their classrooms. Therefore as we look for solutions to the problem of moral decline, we should recognize that public education may not be the solution. In fact, as one nationally syndicated columnist has put it, "education may be one of the problems."

The Disappointment of Government

With the tremendous rise in teenage suicide, sociologists are looking to congressionally created national prevention programs for solutions. As Allen Carlson of the Rockford Institute has stated, "they believe government research rather than a return of religion and traditional family life is the answer."

As a nation, we have come to believe that government can resolve all of our social problems. However, it is clear from history that government may change laws and throw money at problems, but they cannot change the way people choose to live and the manner in which they treat one another. It is an often repeated adage but one which bears repeating: morality cannot be legislated.

A perfect example of this is the problem of racism. The United States government has passed numerous laws to protect blacks against racial discrimination. Nevertheless, the government cannot change the way whites and blacks regard one another, and for this reason, racial problems persist. For the world to change, the change must begin within each individual.

For years now, the state has poured billions of dollars into welfare programs in hopes of wiping out poverty, poor housing, and unemployment. Nevertheless, no governmental institution can force the middle and upper classes of society to have more compassion toward the poor. The government cannot require its people voluntarily to lend a hand and care for the destitute in our land. Hence, poverty and homelessness continue to plague us.

It appears that virtually the entire nation believes government can solve our country's drug problem. If we hire enough law enforcement officials and permanently incarcerate those who sell the drugs, at some point we will have a drug-free society. Our government officials have failed to realize that kids leading meaningless, empty lives will try anything to fill the void. Even if drugs were completely eliminated from the streets, these same kids would sniff glue, steal prescription drugs, or turn to alcohol.

Government is good when it seeks to ensure justice and liberty, protection and security for every one of its citizens regardless of race, creed, sex, or color. That is, after all, its responsibility. However, government should not hold itself out as society's savior—all it will accomplish in the role of quasi-savior will be to pass more laws and create more bureaucratic agencies and end up simply throwing money at the symptoms of our problems Any perceptive citizen—Republican or Democrat—must acknowledge that the powerful institution of government becomes powerless when it takes on the charge of correcting the root problems of our society's ills. That is not and can never be its job.

The Forgotten God

Many years ago, in its infancy, *Time* magazine asked several hundred prominent philosophers and theologians to write a response to the question "What is Wrong with the World?" G. K. Chesterton, the celebrated English journalist and novelist, was among those contacted. He wrote back:

> Gentlemen,
>> In response to your question, "What is Wrong with the
>> World?" I am,
>>>> Sincerely,
>>>> G. K. Chesterton

I would imagine the editors of *Time*, expecting perhaps to receive a more detailed response, were perplexed to receive just the two words "*I am.*" Chesterton, however, went straight to the heart of the matter. He understood that man was the problem, nothing else.

With the production of the first atomic bomb, Albert Einstein was asked if he thought it would bring peace to the world. Einstein responded somberly, "The world will never experience peace because man lives in the world."

The philosopher Will Durant once asked, "Why is it that such a simple paradise never comes? Why is it that utopia never arrives on the map? The answer, because of greed and luxury. Men seldom desire anything unless it belongs to others."

C. S. Lewis made the observation that mankind, engaged in self-centered deeds, loses its capacity to perceive what *good* really means. Vice has no way of understanding virtue. As man yields himself to selfish living, he blunts the very capacities in himself that might have helped him to understand and appreciate that which is good and virtuous. He truly becomes an animal, yet is not even aware of it.

What is wrong with the world? Chesterton's answer still stands: *Man* is the problem.

Who can understand the hearts of men? Who can understand why people live as they do? How is it that some parents physically abuse their children? How is it that two people who are deeply in love, who have sealed that love by taking the vows of marriage, end up hating each other as they file for divorce? How could it be that certain individuals get sexual pleasure viewing children taking part in pornographic films? What is wrong with our world? Is there any way out of this chaos?

What we are faced with is clearly a spiritual problem. Pope John Paul II, in 1985, said that "upon looking at the power struggles and self interest that exist in our world today, we must ask: Is there a solution? The crux of the matter is that man must love God above all else and love his neighbor as himself. The law of God, written in people's hearts and proclaimed by the Church, provides the norms and impulses for the solution, for God's word transcends time. Violence flourishes in lies and needs lies. The greatest lie, the basic falsehood, is to refuse to believe that man has the need to be redeemed from the evil and sin within him."

Dr. John Hallowell concludes his book *Main Currents in Modern Thought* with a solemn warning. "The crisis we find ourselves in is the culmination of modern man's progressive attempt to deny the existence of a transcendent or spiritual reality." The solution, he concludes, lies in the return to "a society that intellectually and spiritually is God-centered rather than man-centered."

In 1981, Alexander Solzehenitsyn received the Templeton Prize in Religion and in his acceptance speech said:

> Over half a century ago, while I was still a child, I recall hearing a number of older people offer the following explanation for the great disasters that had befallen Russia: "Men have forgotten God; that's why all this has happened."
>
> Since then I have spent well-nigh fifty years working on the history of our revolution; in the process I have read hundreds of books, collected hundreds of personal testimonies, and have already contributed eight volumes of my own toward the effort of clearing away the rubble left by the upheaval. But if I were asked today to formulate as concisely as possible the main cause of the ruinous revolution that swallowed up some sixty million of our people, I could not put it more accurately than to repeat: *Men have forgotten God.*

The Difference God Makes

Human beings have a basic heart problem. As the Old Testament prophet Jeremiah put it, "the heart of man is more deceitful than all else and is desperately sick; who can understand it?" For many years I wondered if God could really make a difference in a person's life. Could He really transform hate into love, selfishness into unselfishness, meanness into kindness, and unhappiness into joy? Could He heal the human heart?

"Death called to us from every direction. It was in the air we breathed, it was the chief topic of our conversation." So begins one of the most vivid accounts of God actually transforming the hearts of men. During World War II, Dr. Ernest Gordon, a former chaplain at Princeton University who had been stationed in the Pacific theater, was captured and placed in a Japanese labor prison camp. He recounts in a remarkable book, *Through the Valley of Kwai,* the inhumane living conditions to which the prisoners were subjected:

As conditions steadily worsened, as starvation, exhaustion and disease took an ever-growing toll, the atmosphere in which we lived was increasingly poisoned by selfishness, hatred, and fear. We were slipping rapidly down the scale of degradation. You could say we lived by the rule of the jungle, I look after myself and to hell with everyone else. Consequently, the weak were trampled underfoot, the sick ignored and resented, the dead forgotten. When a man lay dying, we had no word of mercy. When he cried out for help, we averted our heads. Men cursed the Japanese, their neighbors, themselves, and God. We had no church, no chaplains, no services. Many had turned to religion as a crutch. But the crutch had not supported them, so they had thrown it away. We had long since resigned ourselves to being derelicts, motivated by hate.

Then two incidents took place that completely transformed this death camp. One of the men in the camp, a very devout Christian by the name of Angus, sacrificed himself for one of his friends. This friend had contracted a disease and was surely to die. Someone stole his blanket and Angus gave him his own. Every mealtime, Angus would show up to draw his ration, but he wouldn't eat it. He would take it to his friend and make him eat it. Over time, the friend got better but Angus finally collapsed, slumped down, and died from starvation.

During the next few days on my visits to the latrine I heard other

prisoners discussing Angus' sacrifice. The story of what he had
done was spreading rapidly throughout the camp. Evidently it had
fired the imagination. He had given us a shining example of the way
we ought to live, even if we did not.

One that went the rounds soon after concerned another Argyll. He
was in a work detail on the railroad.

The day's work had ended; tools were being counted. When the
party was about to be dismissed the Japanese guard declared that a
shovel was missing. He insisted someone had stolen it to sell to the
Thais. He strode up and down in front of the men, ranting and
denouncing them for their wickedness, their stupidity, and most
unforgivable of all, their ingratitude of the Emperor.

Screaming in broken English, he demanded that the guilty one
step forward to take his punishment. No one moved. The guard's
rage reached new heights of violence.

"All die! All die!" he shrieked.

To show that he meant what he said, he pulled back the bolt, put
the rifle to his shoulder, and looked down the sights, ready to fire at
the first man he saw at the end of them.

At that moment the Argyll stepped forward, stood stiffly to attention, and said calmly, "I did it."

The guard unleashed all his whipped-up hatred, he kicked the
hapless prisoner and beat him with his fists. Still the Argyll stood
rigidly at attention. The blood was streaming down his face, but he
made no sound. His silence goaded the guard to an excess of rage.
He seized his rifle by the barrel and lifted it high over his head. With
a final howl he brought the butt down on the skull of the Argyll,
who sank limply to the ground and did not move. Although it was
perfectly evident that he was dead, the guard continued to beat him
and stopped only when exhausted.

The men of the work detail picked up their comrade's body,
shouldered their tools, and marched back to camp. When the tools
were counted again at the guardhouse no shovel was missing.

News of similar conduct began to reach our ears from other
camps. One incident concerned an Aussie private who had been
caught outside the fence while trying to obtain medicine from the

Thais for his sick friends. He was summarily tried and sentenced to death.

On the morning set for his execution he marched cheerfully along between his guards to the parade ground. The Japanese were out in full force to observe the scene. The Aussie was permitted to have his commanding officer and a chaplain in attendance as witnesses. The party came to a halt. The C.O. and the chaplain were waved to one side. The Aussie was left standing alone.

Calmly, he surveyed his executioners. Then he drew a small copy of the New Testament from a pocket of his raged shorts. He read a passage unhurriedly to himself. His lips moved but no sound came from them.

What that passage was, no one will ever know. I cannot help wondering , however, if it were not those words addressed by Jesus to his disciples in the Upper Room:

Let not your heart be troubled:
Ye believe in God, believe also in me.
In my Father's house are many mansions:
If it were not so, I would have told you,
I will come again, and receive you unto myself;
That where I am, there ye may be also.
... Peace I leave with you,
My peace I give unto you:
Not as the world giveth, give I unto you.
Let not your heart be troubled,
Neither let it be afraid.

He finished reading, returned his New Testament to his pocket, looked up, and saw the agitated face of his chaplain. He smiled, waved to him, and called out, "Cheer up, Padre. It isn't as bad as all that. I'll be all right."

He nodded to his executioner as a sign that he was ready. Then he knelt down, and bent his head forward to expose his neck.

The Samurai sword flashed in the sunlight.

One evening an Australian sergeant whom I had never met before came to see me. We squatted on the ground in front of my shack and talked of this and that. He had something on his mind, but it took him a little time before he could bring himself to speak of it. Finally he said, "My cobbers and I have been talking things over. We got to wondering if maybe there isn't something in this Christianity business after all—something we haven't understood aright in the past."

"Yes sir, my cobbers and I have given this a lot of thought. We've seen the worst there is—right? Now we feel there must be something better—somewhere. So we want to have another go at this Christianity—to find out if it's absolute 'dingo' or not."

The logical place for me to begin now, I reflected, was with the New Testament, as the only record of his life and teaching available.

I had a Bible. It was an old one which had been given to me by a kindly "other rank," who wished to lighten his pack as he set out for a trip farther up-country. It was well-thumbed, torn, and patched, and covered with the oilskin of a gas cape. There were no references, explanations, or annotations.

That Bible was all I had to draw on when I faced the group the next evening in the bamboo grove. I was not a little dismayed to see that there were several dozen of them.

They were waiting for me in respectful silence. But their faces held a look of warning which plainly said, "We'll tolerate you, chum, so long as you don't try waffling." (Waffling is the gentle art of evading the issue or of making a half-lie take the place of the truth.)

They were very kind, those cobbers. When they began to talk they spoke freely of their own inner questioning. They gave their honest views about life on earth, its object and the life hereafter. They were seeking a truth they would be able to comprehend with the heart as well as the mind. When the meeting ended, I knew I could go on.

At each successive gathering the numbers grew. There were new faces, more and more and more pairs of eyes to look questioningly into mine. I expounded the New Testament in their language, keeping one lesson ahead of them.

Through our readings and our discussions we came to know Jesus. He was one of us. He would understand our problems because they were the sort of problems he had faced himself. Like us, he often had no place to lay his head, no food for his belly, no friends in high places.

"Love suffereth long and is kind."

The doctrines we worked out were meaningful to us. We approached God through Jesus the carpenter of Nazareth, the incarnate word. Such an approach seemed logical, for he declared himself by his actions to be full of grace and truth.

We arrived at our understanding of God's ways not one by one, but together. In the fellowship of freedom and love we found truth, and with truth a wonderful sense of unity, of harmony, of peace.

We were developing a keener insight into life and its complexities. We were learning what it means to be alive—to be human. As we became more aware of our responsibility to God the Father, we realized that we were put in this world not to be served but to serve. This truth touched and influenced many of us to some degree, even those who shunned any religious quest. There was a general reawakening. Men began to smile—even laugh—and to sing.

Along with our awakening came a spontaneous hunger for education. Exhausted as men were by their work on the railroad, and subjected as they were daily to cruelties and deprivations in the camp, their minds were very much alive. To satisfy this hunger, a jungle university was established. Perhaps "established" is too grand a word, for it was a university without lecture halls, without trustees or an admissions office, without a campus. Classes were held anywhere, at any time.

It was clear that the quest for meaning, the religious search, and the hunger for knowledge all go hand in hand.

The leaven was spreading. We were spiritually armed. We had a will to life rather than a will to death.

The first communion which I attended was memorable. With expectant hearts men had come to receive the strength that only God could give. The elements were of our daily life—rice baked into the form of bread, and fermented ice water. The solemn word of the fraction were said: "Who the same night in which He was betrayed, took bread and when he had blessed and given thanks he broke it and said, 'Take, this is my body which is broken for you, this do in remembrance of me.'"

We broke the bread as it was passed to us and then passed it to our neighbor.

The elements were returned to the Table, a prayer of Thanksgiving said, a hymn sung, and a blessing given. We slipped quietly away into the singing silence of the night, cherishing as we did so our experience of the communion of saints. The Holy Spirit had made us one with our neighbors, one with those at home, one with the faithful in every land, in every age, one with the disciples.

All the while our own future was unpredictable. We didn't know what the Japanese might have in store for us. We had no assurance that we would ever again see home or those we loved.

Gordon concludes this extraordinary and moving testimony, saying that "whatever happened, we knew that Jesus our leader would never fail us. As he had been faithful to his disciples in the first century, he would be faithful to us in the twentieth."

The Bible has God for its author, salvation for its end, and truth without any mixture of error for its matter.

John Locke

Is The Bible Valid?

For centuries, Christians have held the belief that the Bible is God's chief means of communicating His thoughts to mankind. Within the Old and New Testaments we find not only God's divine principles for living, but a detailed and well preserved record of Jewish history, the lives of the Prophets, the life of Jesus, and life in the early Christian Church. It is clear that this written revelation exists to be passed on to and remembered by each succeeding generation. Nevertheless, the question that will always plague the skeptical mind remains: Why should I believe that this book is God's written revelation?

In the life of Jesus, we see that God is personal and relational, and that it is not His desire to leave His creatures in isolation or darkness. In Jesus—in that mysterious period in history when God became man—we see God's clear intention to reveal Himself. As Malcolm Muggeridge testifies, "I knew from a very early age—how I cannot tell—that the New Testament contained the key how to live. I somehow knew it to be our only light in a dark world. Not just that Jesus was a good man, and his moral precepts greatly to be admired . . . I understood that Jesus could not be turned into just a great man without diminishing him to the point that Christianity became too trivial to be taken seriously. He was God or he was nothing."

While we may have come to recognize the presence of an infinite, personal God in the universe, a critical question remains: Has God chosen the written words of the Bible as His means of revelation and instruction?

Do you not agree that if God chose to communicate with His creatures He would have chosen to do so in a way that would remain free from error? Do you not agree that He would want Himself to be clearly understood?

Do you think God, who is all-powerful, is capable of having specially appointed men write out his words for Him so that the world would have, in effect, a divinely inspired letter from God? I am not saying that you should accept that He has done this, I am only asking "Is He capable?" Is He capable, as the Bible puts it, of having "men moved by the Holy Spirit" write out His words? Obviously, they had to have been specially appointed men, such as Jeremiah the prophet, to whom God said "take a scroll and write on it all the words which I have spoken to you." Again, the question remains is He capable of doing this? If God is all-powerful, the answer must be *Yes.*

If God has chosen to reveal Himself to His people, why would He have chosen the written word as His primary means of communication? Before attempting to explain this, it is important to point out that the written word has not been His *exclusive* method of expression. For example, there are recorded instances in the Bible when God, for certain reasons, chose to speak audibly to Abraham, Moses, Job, and others. Then in the New Testament, we witness the clearest manifestation of God Himself in the person of Jesus Christ. Nevertheless, most of humanity must seek the heart and mind of God through the recorded scriptures.

Why does God speak through the Bible only? Why doesn't God speak to us from heaven as He did with Abraham and Moses? Why can't we in the modern world have this same demonstration from God?

A very difficult question that plagues many non-believers is why doesn't God just simply speak up and let His presence be known. My response must be that if the infinite God spoke to us from heaven, we would be terrorized into loving and listening to Him. Such a direct and demonstrative communication would create a situation whereby God actually forced Himself on mankind. Serving and listening to Him would become compulsory.

This has been beautifully demonstrated in a parable told by the great Danish philosopher Søren Kierkegaard. Kierkegaard tells the story of a powerful king who lived in a magnificent palace that overlooked the city marketplace. One day, as the king was milling about on one of the large terraces of his palace, he observed a beautiful young peasant girl come into the market to purchase some fruits. He was immediately taken by her beauty, her smile, and her kindness. Each day he found himself drawn to his window to wait for her to appear. The young peasant was not aware that each day she was being admired by her powerful king. Finally, one day the king realized he was hopelessly in love with this peasant girl.

At this point, the king knew that he could force her to be his wife, by mere order. Nevertheless, he was wise enough to realize that force could not produce real love. Therefore, he took off his crown and fine clothes and dressed as a peasant, and proceeded into the marketplace, hoping to win her hand by love and not by force. Though she might reject him, he recognized that true love exists only when we choose to love from a condition of freedom.

Author Phillip Yancy in his book *Disappointment With God* observed that God's open demonstration of power in the Old Testament did not encourage spiritual development. In fact, the Israelites in the desert had no need of faith at all. God's clear presence sucked away freedom, making every choice that confronted them a matter of obedience and not faith. As Yancy noted, "God did not play hide-and-seek with the Israelites; they had every proof of His existence you could ask for. But astonishingly—and I could hardly believe this result, even as I read it—God's directness seemed to produce the very opposite of the desired effect. The Israelites responded not with worship and love, but with fear and open rebellion. God's visible presence did nothing to improve lasting faith."

Perhaps it is for this reason that God has chosen not to appear in a manner manifestly divine and capable of convincing the hardest skeptic; but, at the same time, neither has He hidden Himself so that He would not be recognized by those who sincerely sought Him. Through the recorded scriptures, the God of love has revealed Himself. It is His desire to draw us to Himself with a message of love. We must approach Him in faith and from a choice of our own free will.

God dealt with us in the same way as the wise king of the parable dealt with the object of his love—by coming into the world as a man. In doing so, God revealed Himself to us, demonstrated His love for us by laying down His life for us, and we have been left with the written word as testament to that truth.

Moreover, I also believe there are several other logical and imperative reasons for God to employ the written word:

1. Communication is most clearly understood when it is written down. In politics, to take a secular example, when the White House wants to make a statement that will provide little opportunity of being twisted or misinterpreted, they issue a written statement. Politicians generally (and understandably) fear the live press conference, recognizing that they can make an erroneous statement or a diplomatic gaffe that can cause significant political embarrassment.

2. Our laws and court decisions must be recorded because law and doctrine must be objective and verifiable. In the news, one will often hear of a disturbed person attempting to justify a crime such as murder or rape by saying "God told me to do it." However, we can refute such a statement by referring to God's written recorded law in the Bible which prohibits such behavior.

3. Christianity is a historical faith. It is built upon a historical event—the life, death, and resurrection of Jesus Christ. Since history is an interpretation of the past and is based on testimony, history demands that, whenever possible, events and happenings be recorded.

Clearly, the Christian believes that God has spoken and revealed all that we need to know. God's truth becomes clear. It is recorded in the Old and New Testaments. God does not have to add to His written record every century because truth does not change. He does not change. Though society has changed countless times over the centuries, and will change countless more times in the centuries to come, we find comfort in the knowledge that truth, for it to be truth, cannot change.

Many theists are quick to argue that God has revealed Himself through nature; we are able to see His order and handiwork in creation. This is indeed true; however, God's revelation in the natural world is but a subjective revelation where God has demonstrated order and design. The Biblical revelation, on the other hand, provides an objective and personal message from God. I am convinced that the written word is the best and most feasible way for God to communicate with His people.

God knows that society changes and technology changes but truth does not change. He seems to be challenging us, "Pick up the written revelation and check it out for yourself. Or you can deny or ignore it altogether. This is a choice only you can make. I have given you a free will."

History and Archeology

If the Bible is true, then the dates, places, people, and events described in it should be in conformity with historical events and archaeological discovery. They should not contradict one another.

It may be surprising to many of us but the vast number of archaeological discoveries made within the last century have confirmed the validity and historical accuracy of the scriptures. Consider the following statements made by some of the world's leading archaeologists and scholars.

Nelson Glueck

The celebrated Jewish archaeologist, who has spent years on digs in the Middle East, has said, "It may be stated categorically that no archaeological discovery has ever controverted a biblical reference." He went on to comment on "the almost incredibly accurate historical memory of the Bible, and particularly so when it is fortified by archaeological fact."

F. F. Bruce

This archaeologist from the University of Manchester in England has said, "It may be legitimate to say that archaeology has confirmed the New Testament record."

Clark Pinnock

Clark Pinnock, a professor at Regent College, suggests that "there exists no document from the ancient world witnessed by so excellent a set of textual and historical testimonies, and offering so superb an array of historical data on which an intelligent decision may be made. An honest person cannot dismiss a source of this kind. Skepticism regarding the historical credentials of Christianity is based upon an irrational anti-supernatural bias."

William F. Albright

An archaeologist at Johns Hopkins University, William Albright, confirms the growing weight of authority of Biblical accuracy. "The excessive skepticism shown toward the Bible by important historical schools of the eighteenth and nineteenth centuries has been progressively discredited. Discovery after discovery has established the accuracy of innumerable details, and has brought increased recognition to the value of the Bible as a source of history."

Sir William Ramsay

This noted Oxford scholar and archaeologist holds what some may think is a rather radical position concerning Luke's ability as a historian. Ramsay concluded, after 30 years of study, that "Luke is a historian of the first rank; not merely are his statements as fact trustworthy . . . this author should be placed along with the very greatest of historians."

Of this last authority, Sir William Ramsay, it is interesting to note that Ramsay was an atheist, the son of atheists of great wealth, who received his doctorate from Oxford. He committed his entire life to archeology, and was determined to undermine the validity of the Bible. He set out for the Holy Land with the hope of discrediting the Book of Acts. As mentioned in the above paragraph, after years of study, Ramsay declared that Luke, the author of the book of Acts, was exact down to the most minute details. In his diggings and through his study, Ramsay uncovered hundreds of artifacts which confirmed the historicity of the New Testament record, until finally, in one of his books, he revealed that he had become a Christian, shocking the archaeological community.

People often ask, Why are there not more people who wrote about Jesus back during that time, other than the Biblical writers?

In point of fact this was an agrarian society and most of the population could not read or write. They depended on the religious leaders in the community for this. It should not be surprising that since Jesus was such a threat to these religious leaders, we do not find them writing much about Him.

Nevertheless, there were quite a few historians who lived during this time who did write about the life of Christ. Some of these historians were: Cornelius Tacitus, Lucian of Samosata, Tertullion, Thallus, Phlegon, and Justin Martyr. Finally, consider the writings of Flavius Josephus, a historian in the ancient world who wrote several years after the death of Christ:

> Now there was about this time Jesus, a wise man, if it be lawful to call him a man, for he was a doer of wonderful works, a teacher of

such men as receive the truth with pleasure. He drew over to him
both many of the Jews, and many of the Gentiles. He was the Christ,
and when Pilate, at the suggestion of the principal men among us,
had condemned him to the cross, those that loved him at the first did
not forsake him; for he appeared to them alive again the third day;
as the divine prophets had foretold these and ten thousand other
wonderful things concerning Him. And the tribe of Christians so
named from him are not extinct at this day.

Changes Over Time

An architect I know refuses to consider the validity of the Christian faith
and the claims of Christ because he is convinced that the Biblical record has
been tampered with over time. He raises a very important issue: How do we
know that the Bible has not been altered over the past two thousand years?
Prior to the invention of the printing press in the fifteenth century, the
Biblical record was passed down through the ages by handwritten manuscripts. How do we know that the copiers did not embellish or delete a large
portion of the original manuscripts?

We who live in the twentieth century are the fortunate beneficiaries of a
massive number of ancient manuscripts discovered in Palestine over the last
fifty years. These manuscripts are known as the Dead Sea Scrolls.

In 1948, a shepherd stumbled upon a cave full of sealed jars that contained thousands of ancient manuscripts. At the time, a young scholar in the
area, by the name of John Tremor, who was an excellent amateur photogra-
pher, made photographs of the great Isaiah Scroll, which is twenty-four feet
long and ten inches high. He sent prints to Dr. William Albright at John
Hopkins University, a preeminent authority on Biblical archaeology. Albright
later spoke of these scrolls as "the greatest manuscript discovery of modern
times . . . . What an absolutely incredible find! There can happily not be the
slightest doubt in the world about the genuineness of the manuscript." He
went on to date the scrolls at approximately 100 BC.

What is so incredible about the discovery was the manner in which it verified the accuracy of the scriptures that have been passed down to us. The exactness of the Isaiah scroll in comparison with what we have today demonstrates the unusual accuracy of those who copied the scrolls through the centuries.

For instance, in the fifty-third chapter of the Book of Isaiah, which contains one hundred sixty-six words, there are only seventeen letters in question. Of these seventeen, ten are simply a matter of spelling, which does not affect the meaning; four letters are minor stylistic changes, such as conjunctions; and the final three letters in question comprise the word "light," which was added in verse eleven, yet which does not impact the meaning of the passage. As Dr. Norman Geisler has summarized, "Thus, in one chapter of one hundred sixty-six words, there is only one word (three letters) in question. After two thousand years of transmissions, this does not significantly change the meaning of the passage."

As the years have passed, additional discoveries of New Testament manuscripts have turned up and have demonstrated that same "exactness" in transmitted copies. Prior to these discoveries, many liberal theologians believed the New Testament was written in the late second century, and that these writings were myths and legends that had developed during the lengthy interval between Christ's life and the time these accounts were put in writing. These recent archaeological discoveries have shattered the erroneous conclusions concerning New Testament dating by men such as Rudolf Bultman, F. C. Baur, and Rudolf Augustein. Dr. Clark Pinnock, professor of archaeological studies at Regent College, states:

> The early dating of the New Testament documents does not support the theory that legends grew up around the figure of Jesus in absence of historical controls. Paul's letters are firmly dated in the first decades after the death of Christ, and he refers to the eyewitnesses that he knew and talked with. Mark wrote his Gospel a mere thirty years after Jesus died, and he designed it for Christians in Rome who were suffering under Nero's persecution.
> Thirty years is not a very long time. Imagine a person writing

today about the second World War and dreaming up all kinds of events that never happened. He wouldn't get away with it because there are so many around forty-five years later who can still remember those days as if they were yesterday. It is even a shorter period that we are talking about in the case of Mark's Gospel.

Josh McDowell has very effectively demonstrated the accuracy of the New Testament record through the means of a bibliographical test. This test was designed by a secular historian to test the validity of any piece of classical literature. The test is based on two criteria:

1. The time span between the writing of the original manuscript by the original author and the oldest copy we have in our hands today. The shorter this time gap, the more accurate the manuscript.

2. The number of manuscripts (handwritten prior to the invention of the printing press) that we have in our possession today. The larger the number of manuscripts would indicate a greater accuracy of the writings in question.

McDowell compares the bibliographical testing of the New Testament manuscripts with a large number of pieces of classical literature. To highlight a few:

1. Plato lived and wrote between the years 427-347 BC. The oldest copied manuscripts we have in our hands today were copied in 900 AD. This is a one-thousand-two-hundred-fifty year time gap between the original writing and the oldest copy available today. There are only seven handwritten manuscripts of Plato in our possession at this time, yet few scholars in philosophy question the accuracy or validity of Plato's *Republic*.

2. Homer wrote the *Iliad* in 900 BC, with the oldest copy available to us today having been copied in 400 BC. This is a five hundred year gap and there are six hundred forty three handwritten manuscripts in our possession today.

3. The New Testament was written between 40 to 70 AD, with the oldest available handwritten manuscript copied in 125 AD. This is a fifty-five to eighty-five year gap. What is so mind-boggling is that there are over twenty-four-thousand copies of New Testament manuscripts in our possession today.

All of this overwhelming evidence lead Sir Frederick Kenyon, assistant keeper of manuscripts at the British Museum, to announce: "The interval then between the dates of original composition and the earliest extant evidence becomes so small as to be in fact negligible, and the last foundation for any doubt . . . has now been removed. Both the authenticity and the general integrity of the books of the New Testament may be regarded as finally established."

The Biblical scholar Benjamin Warfield said: "If we compare the present state of the New Testament text with that of any other ancient writing, we must declare it to be marvelously correct. Such has been the care with which the New Testament has been copied, a care which has doubtlessly grown out of true reverence for its holy words."

The Authority of Jesus Christ

The evidence, then, indicates that the Bible is not only historically accurate but that it has remained virtually intact for hundreds of years. Nevertheless, the skeptic can still make his stand on the fact that there are many pieces of classical literature and records of history that are valid and accurate. Why should one believe the Bible is the Word of God, and all other writings are but the words of men? What gives the Bible its position of pre-eminence above all other written works?

My response to this is quite simple. I believe the Bible receives its legitimacy from the confirmation given by Jesus Christ. Jesus, the Son of the living God, made it clear that the words He spoke were the authority of God. On several occasions, Christ made it clear that the Holy Scripture was God's word (at that time referring to what we now refer to as the Old Testament) given to specially appointed men to record. He thus confirmed that the written word was God's method of communicating His thoughts to mankind.

Jesus often quoted from the Old Testament. However, He would describe these quotes as coming from the mouth of God by preceding them with the words "God has spoken" or "God has said." He would also refer to the Old Testament as "God's law." Never did He indicate that any of the Old Testament record was inaccurate.

After the resurrection, before His final departure, Jesus appointed special men as apostles, and to them He promised to "guide into all truth" and to "bring to remembrance all that they had seen and heard" while with Him. It was these men who were to write or approve the New Testament. For this reason, the early church did not include any books in the New Testament that did not have this apostolic authority—each book either had to be written by an apostle (which most of them were) or had to be approved by an apostle (as was, for example, the book of Acts, which was approved by the apostle Paul and is a historical account of the life of Christ and the early church).

Therefore, if we are to focus on the issue of proof of the preeminence of the Bible over all other written works, the burden of proof must shift from "Is the Bible the Word of God?" to "Is Jesus who He said He was?" As maintained earlier, the issue of Jesus' identity is pivotal for any person in search of spiritual truth. It is such a crucial issue that Jesus even asked his own followers, "Who do you say that I am?" At this very moment, He asks of each of us, "Who do you say that I am?"

You might be thinking, "Aren't you attempting to prove the Bible with the Bible?" My response is to remind you that the Bible is historically accurate. From the historical record we must decide who this man Jesus is. If we decide that Jesus is God, then we are in no position to question His authority when He tells us that the Bible is the written Word of God. As a wise person once put it to me, "Once you determine who Jesus is all of the questions a skeptic may have can be answered."

When I first began investigating the Bible and its origins, I remember being very impressed by the manner in which the writers, especially in the New Testament, approached their writing. They either wrote as eyewitnesses or as interviewers of those who had been eyewitnesses. Listen to the words of the apostles introducing their subject matter:

Luke

In as much as many have undertaken to compile an account of the things accomplished among us, just as those from the beginning were eyewitnesses and servants of the word have handed them down to us, it seemed fitting for me as well, having investigated everything carefully from the beginning, to write it out for your consecutive order . . . so that you might know the truth.

Peter

For we did not follow cleverly devised tales when we made known to you the power and coming of our Lord Jesus Christ, but we were eyewitnesses of his majesty.

John

What we have seen and heard we proclaim to you . . . .

These men approached their writing just as any conscientious writer would. They clearly desired their work to be intellectually sound, approaching it objectively and rationally. Rarely do you encounter nonrational events—only men desiring to communicate what they have seen and heard. The authority they spoke from was not from themselves but from Jesus Christ.

In conclusion, we should recognize that the Bible provides the means for the infinite God to reveal Himself to finite human beings. Because He is a God of love, it is not surprising that the essence of the Bible reflects that love, as God gives man truth to build his life on. This truth not only provides wise principles for living, but also provides a guideline for personal morality. God warns us that outside of these guidelines lie the forces that destroy personal well-being. Jesus said explicitly that people have a choice of building their lives on God's truth or by following their own desires. He illustrates this choice in His Sermon on the Mount.

Therefore everyone who hears these words of mine, and follows them, may be compared to a wise man, who built his house upon the rock. And the rain descended, and the floods came, and the winds blew, and burst against that house; and yet it did not fall for it had been founded upon the rock.

And everyone who hears these words of mine, and does not follow them, will be like a foolish man, who built his house upon the sand. And the rain descended, and the floods came, and the winds blew, and burst against that house; and it fell, and great was its fall.

Matthew 7:24-27

I believe in Christianity as I believe the sun has risen, not only because I see it, but because by it I see everything else.

C. S. Lewis

The Barriers To Belief

Coming to Christ involves taking a risk. The Christian faith *demands* a decision. In a sense, not to decide could be considered a decision, a decision which ostensibly allows you to stay where you are without taking any risk at all. However, there is nothing more incapacitating than a tortured, undecided mind in the face of truth. Those who do brave the risk and overcome the barriers that lead to faith discover a personal God who will safely guide them in the many paths of life.

I will always remember spending a number of hours carefully explaining to one of my very best friends the dynamics of Christian faith. After addressing various issues, he decided to do nothing. As he reasoned with me, "I am sure that what you have shared with me is the truth, but I am going to stay on the path that I am on." Later, it struck me that what he had actually said was that he recognized that the Christian faith was the truth, but he was going to reject the truth.

As I go back in time, I am appalled at how often I have failed to act upon that which I knew to be the right thing to do. Why do we so often look truth in the eye and then go the other way?

When finally confronted with the choice of Christianity, many people seem to find it much more palatable to come up with excuses (such as, "What about the uneducated in the Third World?" or "What about all the hypocrites I see in the church who say they are Christian but certainly don't live it?") than to say outright that they reject God. The fact of this hit home with me several years ago. A businessman asked that I meet with him to exchange opinions on certain religious issues that interested him. The first week we met I decided to discuss the validity of the Bible. Before I could utter my first sentence, he interrupted and let me know that he was not sure that he even believed God existed. I spent the next hour sharing with him the evidence which I believe points to God's existence. At the end of the hour, he made it clear that I had not convinced him, but that he would like to continue to meet.

A week later, we reconvened, and I gave him my arguments on the validity of the Bible. He appeared interested, if not fascinated, by what I shared, and we agreed to continue to meet.

Several weeks later, as we concluded our session, he startled me by humbly admitting that he really did believe in God, but that he was afraid to give his life to Christ. He was afraid of what others might think, and he feared that being a Christian might affect his career and his social standing. He confided that he was ready to give his life to Christ but that he wanted to be alone with God to make that commitment. He said he would call me to let me know once he had taken a decisive action. That was six years ago and I am still waiting for his call. It's not important that he make the phone call; he must, however, make the decision—there are no two ways about it.

I share this incident because it offers two valuable insights:

1. Pride is primarily what keeps people from giving their lives to Jesus Christ. It is pride in our lives which causes us to fear what other people will think. We fear that a public profession of a belief in God will ruin our lives.

2. Many people choose to use smoke screens to hide the fact that they have chosen to keep God out of their lives. For instance, it

was more palatable for this young businessman to postpone a decision than to say outright I reject God.

The Barrier of Fear

I recently watched a medical documentary on cancer and cancer prevention. In one segment of the presentation a doctor described the various ways women can effectively detect breast cancer. He made it clear that if they would follow certain procedures on a regular basis, they could, more than likely, detect cancer in the early stages and perhaps conquer it through early treatment. In his final remarks, however, he indicated that many women will probably refuse to test themselves because they fear that "they might find cancer."

This illustrates how fear can affect our judgment. When we fear, we often will deny the truth of our circumstances in hopes that if we ignore them or put on rose-colored glasses maybe they will go away.

I remember Burt Lancaster being questioned on the witness stand in his role as a German war criminal in the movie *Judgement at Nuremberg*. The war trials were held just after World War II, at a time when the world was beginning to uncover all the atrocities of the Holocaust. The prosecutor, in questioning Lancaster, wanted to know how the German people could not have known what was happening to the Jews. He responded: "If the German people said they did not know, it was because they did not want to know." The thought of their beloved country being involved in mass exterminations was intolerable. Instead of accepting the hard truth and attempting to stop the Nazi atrocities, many of the German people simply chose to deny the reality of the Holocaust altogether.

Several years ago, I had a lively discussion with a lawyer who had been on former Senator Gary Hart's staff during the 1984 Presidential campaign. Soon after the campaign, he became disillusioned with the whole political scene and left Washington to go into private practice. During the course of our discussion, he made the statement that the American electorate will never elect someone who tells them the hard truth. The modern politician, he stated, either softens the truth or avoids talking about the difficult issues that face us in the belief that to be elected he or she must tell the American people only what they want to hear. A sad but true commentary on the way we deal with most truths.

How strange we humans are. We are afraid to deal with the truth if it is painful or if it is contrary to what we want. We find it easier to go through life denying hard truths and accepting only what is pleasant to our ears. We pour ourselves into the busyness of our comfortable, protected worlds, so that we can distance ourselves from those issues that make us uncomfortable. When it comes to making a serious decision about God and His expectations for our lives, we deal with it just as we deal with our own mortality: "I'll think about it another day."

We must recognize and come to an understanding of this natural tendency that exists in each of us. Fear, unchecked and mismanaged, always leads to denial, and we may find that we unconsciously deny truth its rightful place in our lives because we fear the results it may bring. Either God exists or he doesn't; either Jesus was the Son of God or he wasn't; either the Bible is the Word of God or it isn't; either I am committed to Him or I am not. Such is the hard but simple truth of the matter.

In his best-selling book, *The Road Less Traveled*, Dr. Scott Peck speaks at length of how people deal with fear of pain. He says:

> Fearing the pain involved, almost all of us, to a greater or lesser
> degree, attempt to avoid painful issues. We procrastinate, hoping
> that they will go away. We ignore them, forget them, pretend they
> do not exist.

Ironically, the consequences of our not confronting the painful issues of life, says Peck, is "what makes life difficult." It is what creates in us frustration, fear, loneliness, anxiety, guilt, regret, anger, and despair. Not surprisingly, Dr. Peck, who has a medical degree in psychiatry from Harvard, also says that avoiding painful issues in life is the primary basis of all human emotional and mental illness.

It is therefore crucial we recognize that 1) dedication to truth generally leads to growth and well-being in life, and 2) denial of truth generally leads to difficulty, destruction, and death. Apply this concept to the woman who is afraid to check herself for breast cancer because of the fear of what she might discover. Assuming one day she does in fact contract breast cancer, her failure to have confronted the reality of cancer's possibility in a timely fashion has eventually conquered and destroyed her. Facing the painful truth of cancer's possibility in life and consequently detecting it in its early stages might well have saved her.

Any counselor who works with alcoholics will tell you that the unrecovered alcoholic lives in a world of denial. The alcoholic has become so chronically dependent that he refuses to admit that he has a problem. For this reason, the first step in dealing with alcoholism is to face the truth and admit, "I have a problem—I am an alcoholic." We resist change even when we know the change to be right and good; we would rather remain the same than to face the unknown results which stem from embracing that truth.

There are many people in our society today who have recovered from alcoholism—as well as other addictions and other addictive behavior—and are living full and meaningful lives. At a certain point, these men and women were not afraid to face the painful truth about themselves. Nevertheless, there remain countless numbers of men and women who have lost their jobs, their families, and finally their health, for the simple reason that they refuse to face the truth.

The Barrier of Commitment

Determining whether God exists or does not exist is the most important pursuit in life. Unfortunately, most men and women attempt to avoid the issue and remain neutral. If a person makes no choice, he in effect will have made a choice. If a man deeply in love with a woman asks her to be his wife, and she responds that she is not sure but that she wants to think about it, what has she really said if three years later she is still contemplating this decision? In effect, she has said no by default. In the same way, many have rejected Christ by remaining neutral. On the one hand, they may go to church and profess a belief in God and Jesus. On the other hand the thought of making a total commitment of their life to Christ is unimaginable. They hope to remain comfortable in a neutral, lukewarm position.

The God of the Bible demands a decision. For you to be spiritually complete in life you must make a decision.

I know an attorney who addressed this issue at a breakfast meeting several years ago. This man graduated from Princeton, had been a law clerk for Supreme Court Justice Hugo Black, and today he is president of a major corporation. He has a sharp, analytical mind. For years he was an agnostic, searching for the truth. In his search, he had decided to read the Bible from cover to cover. He told us that morning that after reading the entire Bible, one truth seemed to emerge, "We are either completely with Jesus, or against Jesus, there is no middle ground." After years of searching, he had finally committed his life to Christ.

I am reminded of the words of Sir Hector Hetherington, president of Glasgow University in Scotland:

> There are issues on which it is impossible to be neutral. These issues
> strike right down to the roots of man's existence. And while it is right
> that we should examine the evidence, and make sure that we have all the
> evidence, it is equally right that we ourselves should be accessible to the
> evidence. We cannot live a full life without knowing exactly where we
> stand regarding these fundamental issues of life and destiny. And there-
> fore we must decide ourselves and you must decide yourself.

The Barrier of Anger

We live in a difficult and brutal world. We daily encounter sickness and disease, evil and misfortune. When we experience these things personally, it produces various reactions within us. The most common response is anger, which is rooted in self-centeredness. Anger is my response when I do not get my way. When my wishes are crossed, and circumstances turn out in ways that are contrary to my expectations, I get angry. It can be as inconsequential as someone driving slowly in front of me or as severe as the unexpected death of a loved one. When we get angry, we look for someone to direct our anger towards, and in so many instances, it is directed towards God. Why did He allow this to happen to me? Where was God when I needed Him? I prayed that He would intervene and help me, yet there was nothing but silence. If there is a God, He obviously does not care about me, my business, or my family.

I know a businessman who hates God because he was stricken by a heart attack in the midst of an illustrious career. He believes it is God's fault that he now lives in an impoverished condition. I know another businessman who bristles at any mention of God. He lost his wife to a long painful battle with cancer, and he is embittered towards God because of his wife's suffering.

There are several other men I know who display an obvious anger over the fact that their fathers died while they were still young boys. Others exhibit that same type of bitterness because a parent deserted them during their childhood. There are so many people who have allowed painful circumstances to transform them into angry, bitter individuals. Though someone else may have caused the pain, the resulting anger is eventually directed towards God, for they firmly believe "He should not have allowed this to happen to me."

In the Judeo-Christian tradition, we have grown up being taught that there is a loving God who cares about our well-being. It is out of this perspective that we have somehow come to believe that God owes us a long, healthy life without tragedy. If we personally experience an inconsistency between this belief and our lives, we believe that God has cheated us. It contradicts how we have always regarded Him—God is good and generous. When we suffer disappointment or hurt, many of us lash out at Him to the point of rejecting Him altogether; this is our way of getting back at Him.

It is certainly most puzzling and distressing when we hear of decent people having experienced a tragedy. A question that is often asked in regards to such pain and suffering is, "Why do bad things happen to *good* people?" I must, however, be quick to point out that there is something fundamentally wrong with the framing of such a question. Jesus makes it clear that there are no perfectly good people, for only God is perfectly good. Remember the words of Jeremiah: "the heart of man is more deceitful than all else and is desperately sick; who can understand it?" The question, "Why do bad things happen to *good* people?" should be posed, "Why do bad things happen to *sinful* people?" We are *all* sinners, we are *all* equal in the eyes of God. This Biblical framework provides the true perspective, one which explains why tragedy and evil touch *all* of our lives—whether we believe it is deserved or not.

The Barrier of Death

Finally, we should recognize that we mistakenly regard death as our great enemy. Death is, as Shakespeare described it, "that land from which no traveler will ever return." In the face of the unknown, we come to regard death as the ultimate *tragedy*, and thus the ultimate *fear* that haunts mankind.

Over twenty-five hundred years ago, God revealed through the prophet Isaiah:

> My thoughts are not your thoughts,
>
> neither are your ways My ways,
>
> declares the Lord.
>
> For as the heavens are higher than the earth,
>
> so are My ways higher than your ways,
>
> and My thoughts than your thoughts.

From these words we perceive that though we may see nothing good in tragedy, God does not see as we see. His judgment differs from ours. What might seem good from our point of view, may not be good in the sight of God; what might be tragic in our sight, might be good in God's eyes. Most of us consider a blessed life to be one of comfort and pleasure. It would never occur to us that God could bless a person's life through pain. Nevertheless, I contend that some of God's greatest blessings can come from painful circumstances.

I am powerfully moved by the words of Alexander Solzhenitsyn, who, at the time he wrote them, had just spent ten difficult years in a harsh Russian prison:

> Bless you prison, bless you for being in my life, for it was there lying on rotting prison straw, that I came to realize that the object of life is not prosperity, as I was made to believe, but it is the maturing of the soul.

Clearly, Solzhenitsyn is telling us that God is more interested in the condition of our soul and our character than He is in our comfort and our pleasure. For this reason, if necessary, He uses humbling failures and painful circumstances to bring about His desired results. In the process, we can grow and mature, or unfortunately, we can turn on God in anger and bitterness.

Finally, I would point out that God never intended for death to be our enemy. Although we see dying as the greatest of all tragedies, from God's perspective, the Bible teaches us, death marks a new beginning. In fact, the Bible clearly teaches that God sent Jesus into the world "to deliver all mankind from the fear of death, which we are otherwise slaves to all of our lives." As the Apostle Paul joyfully declared:

> This perishable must put on the imperishable, and this mortal must put on immortality. But when this perishable will have put on the imperishable, and this mortal will have put on immortality, then will come about the saying that is written. Death is swallowed up in victory. Oh death, where is your victory? Oh death, where is your sting? Thanks be to God, who gives us the victory through our Lord Jesus Christ.

One final question that often emerges when considering the barrier of death, is, Why does death have to be so painful. I am reminded that some of God's greatest servants have died violent, painful deaths. God did not even spare His own Son Jesus from a painful death, but allowed Him to go to the cross in order that His purposes would be accomplished.

We experience pain and immediately and naturally respond to it with anger. In such circumstances, we must attempt to see life from God's perspective—for as sinful, finite creatures, our thinking and perspectives are limited and oftentimes distorted. It is only as we respond to pain in humility and in faith that we are able to grow and develop as total human beings. It is crucial for each of us to understand that it is not what we experience in life that determines what kind of people we become but rather it is how we respond to those experiences.

The Barrier of Hypocrisy

I have noticed over the past few years the great skepticism and division that has resulted from the scandalous events that have taken place in the lives of public figures who proclaim themselves to be Christians. I also often hear of people who have been treated poorly by those who are outspoken Christians. I had one young woman share how, during her childhood, her parents preached the importance of giving her life to Jesus and what a difference it would make in her life. However, she observed in her parent's lives a marriage where love was absent and where anger and bitterness characterized their home life. It is not surprising that she is somewhat cynical about the thought of Christ being the center of her life.

Then there are those who have experienced the aggressive Christian zealot who has tried to cram Jesus down their throats with the threat that they will perish in hell if they are not willing to make a commitment.

Often, people who have experiences similar to those described above will display a cynicism that verges on bitterness. They are angry over the persistent hypocrisy they observe in the church, and are angered even further when they find their lives are being judged by "Christians" who display nothing that resembles Christ-like compassion or kindness.

Someone once told me, "You live out what you believe, the rest is just religious talk." Rest assured that God detests hypocrisy even more than we do. He detests it so utterly because of the damage it does to His name. Though God recognizes that we are all sinful people, He speaks out firmly against those who say one thing, and yet live contrary to what they profess. For this reason, it is not surprising that we become skeptical of Christianity when we see a Christian take an outspoken stand, for example, on moral chastity and marital fidelity, and then is caught in adultery. However, though Christians may fail, Christianity remains true. It is like a principle of mathematics applied incorrectly—regardless of an improper application, the principle or theory remains true. The truth of Christianity does not depend on the behavior of its followers.

Furthermore, the Bible clearly teaches that though we are called on to make moral distinctions, we are not to judge and condemn other people's lives. Jesus said, "I did not come to judge the world but to save it." It is the height of arrogance for any Christian to think that he can assume a responsibility that even Jesus did not assume while He lived on earth. I can truthfully say that those I know who genuinely follow Christ do not look at others with judgmental eyes; rather, they display a love and compassion for all people.

Perhaps the greatest damage of hypocrisy is that it creates the most hostile and the most formidable critics of Christianity and the Church. As outspoken antagonists of Christianity, hoaver, these many anti-Christians have determined their positions without fully understanding the meaning of Biblical Christianity, criticizing the faith they have seen in practice and not as it is in truth. They base their evaluations of Christianity solely on a distorted picture they have developed over a lifetime of witnessing blatant hypocrisy in the lives of many professing Christians. Over time, their hearts become hardened, their minds become closed; because of hypocrisy throughout the Church, they have never been persuaded to take a close look at the real Jesus and the message of true Christianity.

If a person seeking religious truth would take the time to truly search the scriptures and observe the life of Jesus Christ, he would be astounded at what he would discover. Initially, he would find that Christianity is not merely a set of rules as he may have been lead to believe. More significantly, he would next recognize that Christianity is a relationship . . . a relationship with a living, risen Savior. It is out of this relationship that we are given the wisdom to find order and purpose, love and meaning for our lives.

The Barrier of Exclusivity

One of the most difficult teachings in the Bible is that the Christian has exclusive entrance into the kingdom of God. Many people find it hard to believe that Christians would make such an arrogant and heartless claim. Consequently, this issue often causes great division and emotional conflict among those who are open to all religions and those who proclaim that Jesus is the only way to God.

Why does Christianity have to be incompatible with other religions? Are not all religions merely different paths that lead to the same God? What about those who have never heard of Jesus? Should they be held accountable if they are uninformed?

These are emotional, often inflammatory issues. However, it is important to remember that we are trying to determine what is the truth. When one is searching for the truth, it is absolutely essential to cast aside any emotional bias that might prevent us from finding it. As Herbert Schlossberg, author of *Idols For Destruction*, has said, "sentimentality destroys truth. It recognizes that truth is often hard, and therefore tries to soften it." In order to find the truth, we must be as objective as possible.

If you have a hard time with the exclusivity of Christianity, do not be too harsh on those who do not back away from this position. They are following the tenets and the teachings of the Bible. If you want to be upset with someone, it should be Jesus, Peter, or Paul. Jesus said, "I am the way, the truth, and the life; no one comes to the Father, but through Me." (John 14:6) Peter said, "there is salvation in no one else, for there is no other name under heaven that has been given among men by which we must be saved." (Acts 4:12) Paul says "there is one God and one mediator between God and men, the man Jesus Christ." (1 Timothy 2:6)

I must confess that I struggled with this issue for many years, going all the way back to my college days at an Episcopal university where I took a course in comparative religion. Even though I was a Christian, I had difficulty accepting the exclusivity of Christianity. Not too long after graduation, I was listening to a speaker address this subject. As I tried to push my emotions, sentiments, and biases aside, I was struck by the realization that of the five major religions of the world (Islam, Hinduism, Buddhism, Judaism, and Christianity), each claims to be the *truth*. At the same time it also struck me that each of these religions contradict one another. *How could they all be true and yet contradictory?*

Let us look, for instance, at what the four largest of these religions teach about the following: the concept of the deity; the concept of death and afterlife; and, finally, the value of human life. (I am postponing discussion of Judaism until later in the chapter because of its close, virtually inseparable connection with Christianity.)

THE CONCEPT OF THE DEITY

Islam

There is only one god, Allah. Moslems reject Jesus as the son of God, but teach that he was a great prophet. Muhammad was the greatest of all prophets and he was not sinless.

Hinduism

There are several hundred thousand gods, and the number continues to grow.

Buddhism

There is no God. It is an atheistic religion.

Christianity

There exists a triune God, one God in three persons: God the Father, Son, and Holy Spirit.

THE CONCEPT OF DEATH AND THE AFTERLIFE

Islam

Believers go to heaven to be with Allah. In heaven, one will eat, drink, and always be happy.

Hinduism

The Hindu believes in reincarnation. The individual moves up and down the caste system and eventually becomes god-like and one with the cosmic all.

Buddhism

The Buddhist believes in reincarnation, eventually reaching *nirvana*. This is a state where the individual ceases to exist and is finally delivered from the pain of existence.

Christianity

Death is the natural termination of our earthly existence. There will be a final judgment and those who put their trust and faith in Jesus Christ will spend eternity in God's Kingdom. The Resurrection of Christ demonstrated His power over death.

THE VALUE OF HUMAN LIFE

Islam

Women have no value. Moslems believe in Holy Wars in which all who are not Islamic must be massacred as infidels.

Hinduism

Everything is God; consequently, humans are of no more value than animals or plants.

Buddhism

You are an island unto yourself. If you experience suffering, it is because of your Karma—you should be left alone to suffer.

Christianity

Human beings have untold worth, and should be cared for when stricken by disease, injury, and poverty. It is the only religion that values the inherent dignity of man.

I find it humorous that there is such great disagreement over which religion leads to heaven, when in fact none of them agree on what death holds for each of us. It lead theologian Carl Braaten to comment, "If salvation is nothingness, then perhaps Buddha 'saves.' If salvation is the experience of union with the cosmic All, then perhaps Hinduism 'saves.' If salvation consists in being faithful to one's ancestors, then perhaps Shintoism 'saves.' If salvation is being freed from the oppression of the bourgeoisie, then perhaps Marxism 'saves.' If salvation is material well-being, then perhaps capitalism 'saves.' If salvation means 'feeling good,' then perhaps there is salvation, not only outside of Christ, but outside of religion in general. But if salvation is liberation from the power of sin and death, then only Jesus 'saves.'"

Therefore, we are faced with the obvious fact that the major religions of the world, which all claim to be "the truth," are contradictory at the most fundamental level. With what are we then left?

Aristotle observed that any statement violating the law of non-contradiction is nonsense. The law of non-contradiction basically says that two statements that contradict each other cannot both be true. Either one is true or neither is true. The "law of non-contradiction" is simply another way of expressing that *two* cannot equal *four*, that *A* cannot equal *non-A*. Therefore, when you compare various world religions, you cannot argue that there are thousands of gods as the Hindus state, that there is only one god as the Christians contend, and there is no god at all as the Buddhists proclaim. This is nonsense.

Our problem lies in the fact that our sentiments and emotions will not allow us to admit that millions of people in the world could be wrong. Therefore, we distort the truth and make such nonsensical statements as All the major religions lead to the one true god.

The logical, rational seeker of truth must admit that we are left with one of two possibilities. Either one of these religions is true or none of them are true. Any other conclusion would violate the laws of logic.

Assuming that one of the four major world religions is in fact the true religion, how do we determine the valid one? It seems rather obvious that the lives of the central figures in each of these religions should be examined. Were their lives marked by any substantive traits which would lead us to fall to our knees and worship them or their god?

Islam

The main doctrines of the Islamic faith are contained in "The Five Articles of Faith." In summary, these articles state the following:

I. There is only one true God—Allah. He is not a personal God, for he is unknowable. Allah is an all-powerful, sovereign god who will one day judge the world.

II. Angels exist and were, in fact, the means of bringing Allah's message to Muhammad. Every person has two angels assigned to him. One records his good deeds and the other his bad deeds.

III. There are four inspired books of Scripture: The Torah of Moses, the Psalms of David, the Gospel of Jesus Christ, and the Koran. Muslim scholars clearly believe that the first three works have been corrupted by the Jews and Christians, and since the Koran is the last and greatest of these works, it is the final authority.

IV. The six great prophets are Adam, Noah, Abraham, Moses, Jesus, and Muhammad. Since Muhammad is the last prophet, he is the greatest.

V. There will be a final judgement during the Last Days. Those who follow Muhammad will go to Paradise, a place of eternal pleasure.

Muhammad, the founder of the Islamic religion, was born in Mecca in 570 A.D., and was orphaned at an early age. When he turned twenty-five, he married a forty year old woman of great wealth, who bore him six children. It was through this marriage that he obtained the financial resources which allowed him to engage successfully in business and commerce.

Soon after he was married, he showed signs of a religious disposition. He went into the wilderness and retired into caves for meditation. It was during these reclusive periods that he claimed to receive divine dreams and visions. In 610 AD, he shared with his friends and family members that he had received a vision from a majestic being, whom he later identified as Gabriel. In this vision, Muhammad was told that "you are the Messenger of God." Until his death he proclaimed frequently that he received revelations from God. In 650 AD, these revelations were collected and written in the Koran, the book which the Muslims regard as the very words of God.

Twelve years after his first revelation, Muhammad had approximately seventy-five followers scattered around the region of Mecca. At this time he decided to move them all to the city of Medina. From Medina, he and his clan would raid caravans which were on their way to Syria. During these raids, Muhammad and his men would loot and rob the caravans and rape the women. In 624 AD, he lead three hundred fifteen men on an attack of a wealthy Meccan caravan that was making its return from Syria.

This attack angered Abu Jahl, the head of a large Meccan clan, who was tired of Muhammad's incessant raids. Abu Jahl lead a force of eight hundred men to teach Muhammad a lesson. On March 24, 624 AD, the two forces confronted each other in battle. In the ensuing fight, forty-five Meccans were killed, including Abu Jahl, and seventy men were taken captive. At the same time, only fourteen Muslims were killed, and the battle quickly turned into a rout. For Muhammad, this was divine confirmation of his status as a prophet.

At the same time, all those in Medina who had satirized his divine position, were assassinated. Consequently, Muhammad found himself and his position greatly strengthened. Over the next eight years, he gained significant military victories, eventually conquering the great city of Mecca. As he conquered various tribes, the people were told, "believe or die." At this point he was the most powerful man in the Arab world. He died in 632 AD, at the age of sixty-two.

Muslims proclaim that prophets are "Messengers of God" who cannot lie. One real conflict that comparative religion scholars must contend with is the Muslim belief that Jesus was a great prophet and that Muhammad was the greatest of all prophets. Muslims must confront the historical fact that Jesus did not claim to be a prophet but rather the son of the living God. In fact, it was because of this claim that He was crucified. If Jesus was a prophet who couldn't lie, yet who said he was the son of God, how can the Muslim faith reconcile these two positions?

Another problem presented in the Islamic faith is the conduct of Muhammad. For example, at one point during his life, he seduced and stole his daughter-in-law from his adopted son and made her his wife. He justified this action by saying it was commanded of him by Allah. In assessing the "truth" of Islam, we must note that there is no evidence even purporting to back up Muhammad's claim to be God's messenger. Many scholars have argued that men and women were not drawn to Muhammad because they recognized him as speaking the truth, but because they feared for their lives. He was a mighty warrior who propagated a new religion by force. It is not too difficult to win converts when the alternative is to lose your head.

Hinduism

Hinduism, which has developed over a four thousand year period, does not have a single founder or creed, but is a religion of practices and beliefs.

Hinduism is built around the caste system. Caste refers to an individual's class and station in life. A person's commitment to the Hindu Dharma (the ideal way of life) will determine that person's caste in the next life. A trans-migration of the soul occurs at death (reincarnation) where the soul passes from one body to another body as determined by the person's actions, or karma, during life. The highest state one can attain is to become a god. This explains why the number of deities in the Hindu religion reaches into the hundreds of thousands and continues to grow.

One can move up the caste system in one of three ways: the way of good works, the way of knowledge, or the way of devotion. These are summarized as follows:

I. The Way of Works. This consists of carrying out certain pre-scribed religious ceremonies and duties.

II. The Way of Knowledge. This is achieved by meditation, where one learns that human suffering is a result of ignorance. Man needs to learn that he is not an individual person, but a part of the whole, the Brahmin.

III. The Way of Devotion. This is a devotion to some chosen deity and is reflected in acts of worship. Out of the love for this deity, the person will also attempt to demonstrate love in all human relationships.

One of the principal problems with Hinduism is its sheer irrationality. For instance, if a person does not perform the right works, gain the right knowledge, or manifest the right devotion, his soul may transmigrate into a plant, a rock, or an insect. (In some Hindu sects, if a woman is not willing to submit to the advances of her guru, she may come back as a shrub!) Yet, how can a rock or a shrub or an insect attain right knowledge or be sufficiently devoted to a deity to move back up the caste system?

A second major problem involves the complete absence of self-worth and value of human life. In Hinduism, human beings are of no more value than a rat. In fact, the United Nations reported several years ago that India grows enough grain to feed its entire population with enough surplus left over to export to other countries. That same report indicated, however, that one-third to one-half of their annual grain crop is eaten by rats. The United Nations further indicated that there are now in India five times more rats than there are people. They refuse to kill these rats because their Hindu faith teaches that these rats may be their reincarnated ancestors. Furthermore, they refuse to spray their crops because they fear they might be killing ancestors whose souls might have transmigrated into the body of an insect. They eat no beef because the cow is also sacred. Consequently, children in India are allowed to starve to death and millions of adults go hungry as the rat, insect, and cow populations flourish.

Finally, when he does encounter human suffering, a Hindu has no encouragement to get involved, for suffering just happens to be that individual's karma or fate. An individual who is poor, injured, in pain, or even dying must be avoided simply because this is his karma, the inevitable result of a previous life.

Buddhism

Siddhartha Gautama, the Buddha or "Enlightened One," was the founder of the Buddhist religion. He lived from 560 to 480 BC in northern India. Legend has it that his mother, Maya, dreamed of a white elephant that entered her womb and caused her to conceive a child. Ten months later she delivered a son into the world, and seven days later she died.

Prince Siddhartha's father, seeking to keep his son from the culture's mystical religious practices, encouraged him to indulge in all the pleasures of life. He was married at age sixteen and his wife conceived and bore him a son. His father, a wealthy and powerful man, opened the door for a position of political leadership.

It was soon after his son was born that Siddhartha took a fateful chariot ride outside his father's palace. For the first time he witnessed the painful suffering of the general population of India. Overwhelmed by this experience, he considered renouncing his position of power and wealth. He finally decided that he must abandon his wife and son to pursue the life of a religious ascetic and became a recluse.

For six years, he sat at the feet of many teachers, yet failed to find the enlightenment he was seeking. He resolved therefore to sit in meditation until attaining "enlightenment." He sat one evening under a pipal tree and began to meditate. At dawn, Siddhartha declared that he had been transformed into the "Enlightened One" and was now the Supreme Buddha.

The Buddha taught for 45 years and won many converts and disciples by building all his teachings around the issue of suffering. This was particularly important to the crowds he spoke to because for them suffering was a way of life. The foundation of Buddhist teachings are the Four Noble Truths, which affirm the following:

First Noble Truth—life is full of pain and suffering.

Second Noble Truth—craving for the pleasures of life is what causes suffering.

Third Noble Truth—the way to rid your life of suffering is to extinguish your cravings and passions.

Fourth Noble Truth—follow the eightfold path.

The eightfold path provides moral direction for mankind. It teaches that you must renounce the pleasures of your senses; you must have right speech; you should not destroy any living creature; you must earn your living in a way which will harm no one; you must exert the proper effort; you must employ the right motivation; you must experience the suitable type of contemplation; and you must enter the four degrees of meditation.

By following the eightfold path, a person can be delivered from a future life of suffering. At death, one is reincarnated and, as in Hinduism, will return to this life in either a better or worse state, depending on how well one followed the eightfold path in his previous life. The ultimate goal is to achieve *nirvana*, which means "nothingness." *Nirvana* occurs when a person reaches the point where the soul ceases to exist and consequently escapes the endless cycle of reincarnation and suffering.

Buddhism is an atheistic religion. Buddhists do not believe in god or a spiritual world. Therefore, when one says that all religions lead to the same god, they should not include Buddhism, which clearly denies the existence of a supreme being.

Such being the case, a certain dilemma exists regarding the Buddha's authority. Both Muhammad and Jesus maintained that their authority was from above, from God. If, as the Buddhist faith holds, there is no god, then from whence did the Buddha's revelation and authority come? If the Buddha did not receive his teaching from god, then it follows that his doctrine must have come from the reason of man.

Buddhism does not celebrate and revere the intrinsic value and worth of human life. Dr. Ron Carlson, president of Christian Ministries International, was on the Cambodian border in Thailand several years ago where there were four hundred thousand refuges with no place to go. They were suffering deeply from hunger, malnutrition, and all types of sickness and disease. In this Buddhist country of Thailand, Dr. Carlson noted that there were no Buddhist doctors, nurses, or volunteers to care for their suffering Buddhist brothers. Dr. Carlson approached the individual in charge of the monumental task of caring for these people and asked, "Why are there no Buddhist organizations here caring for their Buddhist brothers?" He responded, "Ron, have you ever seen what Buddhism can do to a nation or a people? Buddha taught that each man should be an island unto himself. If someone is suffering, that is their fate, and you are not to interfere." The man went on to point out that the only people and organizations present were Christian.

Christianity

To address the evidence which points to the divinity and authority of Jesus, I refer you back to Chapter Three, "Does God Have A Name?"

However, in concluding this discussion, it might be instructive to point out several of the primary teachings of Jesus, which when placed next to the teachings of Islam, Hinduism, and Buddhism set Christianity apart.

Jesus Christ is the only figure in each of the four religions who actually claims to be God. In one instance, for example, He says, "If you have seen me, you have seen God the Father." (John 14: 9) We are left with the option of either believing this claim to be true or believing it to be false. If it is true, then Jesus is in fact the risen and living Savior. We then must decide if we will submit our lives to Him. If he lied or was a deluded paranoid, then Christianity is not a legitimate faith and Christians are fools who should be pitied.

Unlike the other three major religions, Christianity holds up love and the value of human life as its central teaching. In fact, the Bible teaches that God so loved mankind, that He gave His only son, Jesus Christ, to be sacrificed for the sake of our eternal well-being. Jesus wept over human suffering and cared for and healed those He encountered. He taught that all human beings have intrinsic worth and should be treated with dignity. He also taught that men and women are of equal worth and value.

The final and possibly the most important point of departure between Christianity and all other world religions is the fact that Jesus Christ offers a personal, loving relationship between Himself and His followers. As Ravi Zacharias, a former Hindu and a scholar in the field of world religions, has observed:

> Buddha never talks about having a personal relationship with him or with god. You will never hear of Allah as a personal god being related to you. Hinduism never ever talks of a loving god. Christianity is the only unique faith . . . that offers an eternal God with a personal relationship, who gives you the strength to be truly free.

Judaism

Judaism has not been discussed to this point because of its intimate connection with Christianity. Both Jews and Christians believe in the teachings of the Old Testament. However, there is a significant divergence in belief over the person of Jesus Christ: Jews continue to wait for their Messiah, while Christians contend He has already appeared in history.

Though some may contend they are similar religions because they both worship God, it is important to recognize Judaism and Christianity are actually two conflicting religions which cannot be reconciled without violating the law of non-contradiction. Either Jesus Christ spoke the truth as the Son of God, and Christianity is thus the true faith of God, or Jesus Christ was a liar and a pathetic fraud and certainly not the Messiah. Should this be the case, Judaism makes a strong case that their Messiah could return any day.

I have met quite a few Jews who have converted over to Christianity. One particular individual whom I have had the opportunity to get to know quite well said he was shocked to discover the Old Testament prophecies that point to the coming of the Jewish Messiah are in fact fulfilled in the person of Jesus Christ. Among these prophecies are:

1. The Jewish Messiah is to be born in Bethlehem. In the Old Testament, in the book of Micah (Chapter 5, verse 2), it says, "But as for you Bethlehem, too little to be of the clans of Judah, from you One will go forth for Me to be ruler in Israel."

2. The Jewish Messiah is to be born of a virgin. In the Old Testament book of Isaiah (Chapter 7, verse 14), it states, "Therefore the Lord Himself will give you a sign: Behold, a virgin will be with child and bear a son, and she will call His name Immanuel."

3. The Jewish Messiah will bear the sins of man on his body. Again, in the book of Isaiah (Chapter 53, verse 6) it says, "But the Lord has caused the iniquity of us all to fall on Him."

I concur with my Jewish friend; the Old Testament prophecies do indeed point to the Messiah. Jews today wait, mistakenly, I believe, on a Messiah who will set them free from their oppressors when, in point of fact, Jesus Christ, their Messiah, has already come to deliver them. What they also fail to recognize is that Jesus, their Messiah, came to deliver *all men*—not just Jews—from sin and destruction.

Those Who Have Not Heard

It is legitimate to ask about the person who never hears of Jesus Christ, and therefore has no opportunity to respond to Him. What happens to this person? Though this is a most difficult question, the Bible gives insight into this issue when Paul says in Romans 2:12-16:

For all who have sinned without the Law will also perish without the Law, and all who have sinned under the Law will be judged by the Law; for not the hearers of the Law are just before God, but the doers of the law will be justified. For when Gentiles who do not have the Law do instinctively the things of the Law, these not having the Law are a law to themselves, in that they show the work of the Law written in their hearts, their conscience bearing witness, and their thoughts alternately accusing or else defending them, on the day when, according to my gospel, God will judge the secrets of men through Christ Jesus.

It is clear that God in any and all events will be fair because of His uncompromising commitment to justice. All His decisions and judgments are just, and we as human beings are in no position to second guess them. The prophet Isaiah worded it well when he humbly acknowledged, "But now, O' Lord, Thou art our Father, and we are clay, and Thou our potter; and all of us are the work of Thy hand . . . . Will the clay say to the potter, 'What are you doing?' Or the thing you are making say, 'He has no hands?'" (Isaiah 64:8, 45:9)

Some believe that God can reveal Himself to people through general revelation—which is the light that is obvious to every human being—and consequently evoke repentance and faith (though the person may have never heard of Jesus). Those who take this position contend that the uninformed will have their sins forgiven, and they support their position with Peter's statement in

Acts (10:35), "in every nation the man who fears Him and does what is right, is welcome to Him."

James I. Packer, the noted author and theologian, has declared that this very well may be true. He says "if ever it is true, such worshippers will learn in heaven that they were saved by Christ's death and that their hearts were renewed by the Holy Spirit . . . . Christians since the second century have hoped so, and perhaps Socrates and Plato are in this happy state even now—who knows?

"We have no warrant to expect that God will act thus in any single case where the gospel is not known or understood. If we are wise, we shall not spend much time mulling over this notion. Dealing with these people is God's business: He is just, and also merciful, and when we learn, as one day we shall, how He has treated them, we shall have no cause to complain."

In his book *The Quest for Faith*, Stephen Evans points out that there are many people, "who because of the circumstances of their lives are prevented from hearing about God." He continues, "We may be confident that God will treat such people lovingly and justly. What is crucial to remember is that God will hold you responsible for the evidence and opportunities which were available to you as an individual. It is not your responsibility to decide for those in radically different circumstances."

Conquering Our Stubborn Hearts

I suspect there are many men and women who are intellectually prepared and emotionally eager to make a commitment to Jesus Christ yet who will nonetheless turn away at the last minute. As we have seen, it is far more tolerable to give excuses for a failure to receive Jesus Christ than to honestly admit, "In spite of what I feel in my heart and what I know in my mind to be true, I still have decided to reject God."

Does believing in God mean that we won't be able to do what we want? Is this not the heart of the matter? We become suspicious of God and believe that He wants to take everything enjoyable in this life away from us. With this as our perspective it shouldn't be too surprising that a strong case can be made for living without Him. Don't we choose to live without God because we want to have our own way—because we have stubborn hearts?

Barriers to belief will inevitably surface when an individual is considering a commitment to Jesus Christ. Not to acknowledge the strength of these barriers—to simply sidestep them—is to invite and encourage a shallow faith. It takes courage to confront these smoke screens and successfully penetrate them to reach the heart of the Christian faith. We must be prepared to address and overcome the issues raised by these barriers—with compassion and with intelligence—if we are to conquer our stubborn hearts.

A father decides the time has finally come to take his son to work with him. Early in the morning, hand in hand, they set off together for the town's drawbridge.

Shortly after they arrive, the father, whose job is to raise and lower the trestle to ensure boats and trains safe passage, receives a warning that a train is fast approaching. As he hustles to take up his station, he realizes, much to his horror, that his son has disappeared from the signal room.

He soon discovers that the boy—his only son, whom he loves beyond words—has fallen into the massive gear system which raises and lowers the bed of the drawbridge. To leave it up would save the boy while killing hundreds on the approaching train; to lower it would spare hundreds of innocent lives but destroy his only son.

As the drawbridge lowers into place, the father must endure the agonizing cries of his little boy.

The train rushes past; many of the passengers, oblivious to the circumstances, wave and smile gaily. Just as quickly as they had come they are now gone, each soon forgetting the bridgemaster and the bridge at his command.

The Heart of Christianity

Everyone has an opinion about God and religion. Everyone in a sense has his or her own personal theology. Therefore, when people gather together and discuss religion, diverse opinions will soon surface.

Eugene Peterson says, "The word 'Christian' means different things to different people. To one person it means a stiff, upright, inflexible way of life, colorless and unbending. To another it means a risky, surprise-filled venture, lived tiptoe at the edge of expectation. If we get our information from the Biblical material, there is no doubt that the Christian life is a dancing, leaping, daring life."

I often wonder how people develop their ideas about God. What has shaped and molded their thoughts so that they eventually arrive at some type of personal belief? I am naturally skeptical of a person's theology when the source of their religious belief is obscure and undefined.

What if the source of our religious belief is wrong? Should that be the case, then our ideas about God will be wrong. René Descartes in his philo-

sophical writings, warns us of becoming "infected with errors" of intellectuals. He says that "whenever they have allowed themselves rashly and
credulously to take up a position in any controversial matter, they try with
the subtlest of arguments to compel us to go along with them."

If a person really wants to know the truth about the Christian God, he
or she should go to the best source available: the Bible. As you will recall,
Jesus confirmed that it was through God's written revelation that the world
could know the truth about God. I believe that God never intended to leave
mankind in the dark. Why would He want to leave us guessing?

What will follow in this chapter is not my opinion of what I think the
Christian faith is, but the Biblical account of the nature of God, the nature
of man, and the nature of life after death.

The Nature of The Biblical God

It is impossible for finite man to fully understand the mind, the purposes, and the magnitude of the infinite God. However, mankind can grasp a
significant part of His nature based on what is revealed in the Bible.
Throughout God's written word, He is described as a holy, righteous, and
loving God:

> God is light and in Him there is no darkness at all.
>
> I John 1:5

> Holy, Holy, Holy, is the Lord of Hosts. The whole earth is full of
> His glory.
>
> Isaiah 6:3

> The Lord is righteous in all His ways
> And kind in all His deeds.
>
> Psalm 145:17

> God loves with an everlasting love.
>
> Jeremiah 31:3

All of Scripture pictures a perfectly holy, perfectly righteous God. As
Dr. Ernest Gordon, the erstwhile chaplain of Princeton University, has said,
"He is the Word, the Principle, the Standard, the Norm of all morality in

every age and place and civilization and university. His son Jesus referred to Himself a the I Am, the Amen of God, the Truth, the Way, the Life, the Light of the World, the Bread of Heaven, the Alpha and Omega."

God, through His word in the Bible, is telling us that the standard He has set for mankind is one of righteousness, truthfulness, and justice. He is a God who is righteous, truthful, and just; in Him there is no darkness. He has established the standard by which man should live, and He follows that standard always because His nature *is* the standard.

The Great Dilemma

A dilemma exists when a Holy God has to deal with unholy man. As discussed in Chapter Five, "Is The Bible Valid," mankind has a nature that is innately self-centered. A nature that the Bible describes as being sinful:

> There is none who does good, there is not even one.
> Romans 3:12

> There is not a righteous man on earth who continually does good and who never sins.
> Ecclesiastes 7:20

> The heart is more deceitful than all else and is desperately sick; who can understand it?
> Jeremiah 17:9

> For all have sinned and fall short of the standard of God.
> Romans 3:23

I remember a good friend challenging me on the assertion that there are none who are righteous, not even one. She asked, "Well, what about my husband?" I had to concur that she is married to one of the finest people I know. I expressed my opinion that there are in fact many good, moral people in the world, according to man's standard of goodness. However, the only standard that actually counts is God's, which is one of holiness and righteousness. According to God's standard of holiness, we all fall short.

Consider that Christ said that if we lust in our hearts after a woman, then in God's eyes we have committed adultery. If we have been angry with our brother, we have in fact committed murder in our hearts.

What we often do not recognize is that God not only looks at our words and actions, but our motives, our thoughts, and our attitudes. He looks at the intentions of the heart. For this reason, the person who thinks He is in good standing with God because He has never murdered, robbed, raped, or committed adultery, should recognize that he may in fact be a murderer, robber, rapist, or adulterer because he has committed these deeds in his heart.

I also think that many people do not understand what the Bible means regarding the word sin. Many people equate sin with various actions, such as smoking, drinking, dancing, or going to R-rated movies. These are not necessarily sinful actions.

Sin is an attitude of the heart that says "I want to have my way. I am going to do what I want to do, regardless of what God says, regardless of who it might hurt." It is this attitude in our hearts that explains why mankind lives the way it does, and why the world is so confused and troubled.

Finally, it is important to understand that we are all born with this sinful nature. Many years ago I had an interesting discussion about the nature of man with a friend. He commented that he had always believed that mankind was basically good, until an event took place involving his little boy. At Christmas, he and his wife had given their son, who was three years old, a brand new tricycle. Not knowing this, his grandparents also gave him a new tricycle. On Christmas morning their little boy found himself the proud owner of two new tricycles. Later that day, as he was playing in the yard, the little boy next door wandered over. He did not own a tricycle and had not received one for Christmas, and therefore, as you would expect, the little neighbor asked if he could ride one of the tricycles. My friend (the father) was watching this all take place through the kitchen window. He watched in disbelief as his son straddled both tricycles and told the neighbor's little boy not to touch either tricycle, but to go home and play with his own toys.

As we discussed this, he shared how he and his wife had always taught their son to be generous and kind. It was only after this event on Christmas morning that he came to the realization that his son, like all other people, had an innate selfishness in his heart. It is what the Bible calls sin.

The Consequence of Sin

God has made it clear that He cannot have a personal nor an eternal relationship with sinful people. God often pictures His relationship with His people as a marriage, and we all recognize that a marriage cannot exist if one partner is faithful and the other is not. God is the faithful partner, but we have chosen to go our own way. Someone has described spiritual adultery as giving the love, devotion, and faithfulness that is due to God, to some other master, be it pleasure, wealth, or fame.

The Bible states clearly that sin causes a separation, a barrier between mankind and God, so that people cannot have a relationship with Him:

But your sin has made a separation between you and your God. And your sinfulness has hidden his face from you so that He does not hear.
Isaiah 59:2

The result of our sin is eternal spiritual separation from God.
Romans 6:23

Though God loves us deeply and hungers for a relationship with us, a barrier of sin exists that must be dealt with. I remember a Christian speaker describing an event in his life as a parent that vividly illustrates man's dilemma. One evening he and his wife were awakened by a loud scream from their two year old son's bedroom. The father bolted from his bed, ran down the hall, and flipped on the light switch. There stood his terrified little boy, his chest pressed against the bars of his baby bed, and his pleading arms extended towards his father. His little boy had gotten sick during the night and had vomited all over the bed. Waking up in his darkened room, covered in his own vomit, the little boy did not fully understand what had happened. As the father approached his son, he realized that his little boy was covered in vomit, and being extremely weak stomached had to turn away from his son. (It was a good thing his wife did not have the same weak stomach!)

As he later reflected upon this event, he understood that this is the very same predicament that God faces with mankind. Though He loves us as His people, He cannot live in the presence of a people who are covered in the sickness of their sin. For this reason, we must be saved from our sin and we must discover the means to be cleansed and forgiven.

Reconciliation

God has always provided the means for mankind to be forgiven of sin, even prior to the coming of Jesus Christ. In the centuries that preceded the life of Jesus, the Jewish people would come to the Temple during Passover. They would confess their sin before God, and then the High Priest would take a spotless lamb and sacrifice it with a knife, sprinkling its blood on the high altar.

The sacrifice of a lamb explains why John the Baptist, upon seeing Jesus approaching from a distance, declared Him to be "the Lamb of God who will take away the sins of the world."

After having spent three years teaching and healing among the people, Jesus performed a miracle that shook all of Palestine. He raised from the dead a man named Lazarus who had been dead for three days and whose body had begun to decay. When Lazarus walked forth from the tomb, the countryside erupted with excitement. People began to flock to hear Jesus and looked to him as their religious leader. They greeted him in great numbers and with tremendous fanfare as he arrived in Jerusalem, mounted humbly, as scripture prophesied, on a donkey. At this point, those in opposition to Christ, the religious leaders, decided it would be necessary to get rid of Him. This lead to a plot in which the Jewish leaders conspired with Judas Iscariot, one of Jesus' twelve disciples. Judas lead the Roman soldiers to Christ in the dark and stillness of the night when the masses would be asleep and unable to resist.

Jesus was taken into custody and tried as a common criminal and a blasphemer. As the now confused and fearful masses looked on, Jesus was beaten, spat upon, whipped, ridiculed, stripped naked, and then crucified on a wooden cross. Crucifixion was the method used by the Roman government to execute criminals. It involved driving spikes through the wrists of the person, as well as driving a single long spike through both feet. The person would hang for hours in excruciating pain and would eventually die.

What is so amazing is that Jesus, after having been treated in such a barbaric and inhumane manner, could look down upon his captors and utter the loving words:

Father, forgive them, for they know not what they are doing.

Luke 23:34

The arrest, trial, and crucifixion of Christ caused many of his Jewish followers to turn away from Him. They had fully expected Him, their Messiah, to overthrow the Romans and be a ruler just as King David had been. They could not understand why He did not use the power He had displayed in all the miracles to defeat those who sought to destroy Him.

However, as Jesus said to Pilate:

My kingdom is not of this world. If My kingdom were of this world, then My servants would be fighting, that I might not be delivered up to the Jews; but as it is, My kingdom is not of this realm.

John 18:36

Jesus hung on the cross for six hours. During the first three hours, the Roman guards gambled for his clothes, he was ridiculed by those in the crowd, and he spoke to the two thieves who had been crucified next to Him. Then at twelve noon, the sky darkened and the countryside became as dark as if it were night. It was at this time that God poured upon Jesus His punishment for the sins of all mankind.

How God transferred mankind's sin to Jesus cannot be fully understood by the human mind. As the Bible explains it:

He made Him who knew no sin to be sin on our behalf.

2 Corinthians 5:21

And He Himself bore our sins in His body on the cross . . . for by His suffering you can be healed.

I Peter 2:22

As Jesus bore the sins of the world on his shoulder, God the Father in His Holiness turned away from His Son and it was at this precise moment that Jesus cried aloud, "My God, My God, why have you forsaken Me?" (Matthew 27:46)

At approximately three o'clock in the afternoon, Jesus uttered, "It is finished." The work He had come to do was complete and He died.

Receiving Forgiveness

The question that remains is how do people have their sins and punishment transferred to Christ? This is a most crucial matter, for in the end it answers the questions: How is mankind reunited with God? How does one become a Christian?

The most relaxed opinion regarding God's forgiveness of sin is that mankind has to do nothing to receive it. All of humanity is forgiven on a blanket basis because of what Jesus accomplished on the cross. Even though this is an inviting thought, it is not supported by the Biblical record. In fact the Bible makes it clear:

God has given us eternal life, and this life is through His Son,
Jesus Christ. He who has the Son has eternal life. He who does not
have the Son does not have eternal life.

1 John 5: 17,18

A second, very common opinion, yet one that is not Biblical, is that
God forgives those who do good deeds. Nowhere does the Bible teach that
good deeds result in God's favor and God's forgiveness. Rather, it teaches
that man cannot possibly be good enough to measure up to God's perfect
standard. It clearly states:

For whoever keeps God's whole law and yet breaks only one of
them, is guilty as if he broke all of it.

James 2:10

Furthermore, the Apostle Paul makes it clear in the second chapter of
Ephesians that man can receive God's forgiveness, "but not as a result of
good works."

A third opinion is that man is forgiven by having the correct beliefs in
God and Jesus. As long as one believes that Jesus is the son of God then
that person will receive God's forgiveness. This, too, is an errant opinion
because the Bible clearly indicates that merely believing in God and Jesus
is not enough. "You believe that God is one. You do well; the demons also
believe, and shudder." (James 2:19)

So what does the Bible reveal about receiving God's forgiveness?
What must one do? The Bible states that a person receives God's forgiveness by grace through faith and trust in Jesus Christ.

For by grace you have been forgiven, through faith . . . .

Ephesians 2: 8

We receive the righteousness of God through faith in Jesus Christ.

Romans 3:22

I do not have a righteousness of my own from following God's law, but that which is through faith in Christ, the righteousness which comes from God on the basis of faith.

Philippians 3:9

I remember the first time I heard this message, that faith rather than works is the source of salvation. I thought it sounded great. However, looking back, I realize how I confused the word *faith* with the word *believe*. Belief is important, certainly; but faith is far more than belief. Faith is a belief which results in action. It involves entrusting my life to Jesus Christ.

For example, assume I awake tomorrow with an unbearable headache and learn that I have a brain tumor. The neurologist with whom I consult, after examining the X rays, tells me that he is convinced that he can cure me, but that it would require a delicate and dangerous operation. At this point I breathe a sigh of relief, for I believe that this doctor can do what he says. However, my belief is worthless unless I act upon that belief. In order to be healed, I must entrust my life into his care and allow him to operate on me. This is also true of God. He cannot forgive me of my sin until I first believe that Jesus Christ is the Son of God, that He died on a cross for me, and that He desires for me to entrust my life to Him. Then it is just as important that I act upon that belief and commit myself to following Him.

If you will recall, sin is an attitude: "I want to have my way, I am going to live the way I want to live." Placing my faith in Christ means turning from that attitude and approaching life with a new one—an attitude of "Lord, I want to do what you want me to do. I want you to have your way in my life. I want to see with your eyes, to think with your mind, and to feel with your heart."

Coming to Jesus Christ in faith is indeed comparable to a marriage relationship. When a man and a woman fall in love and begin to consider marriage, eventually they must consider the costs as well as the benefits. Do I really want to get married? Do I want to give up a single life in which

I can do what I want to do whenever I want to do it? Do I want to give up dating other people? Two people who are going to live out their lives in commitment to one another must consider these questions.

In coming to Jesus Christ you must ask yourself, Do I really want to be a Christian and be publicly identified as one? What will people think? What new responsibilities will I have to take on? Who can do a better job of running my life, God or me?

When a man and woman, after considering the costs of marriage, recognize that they want to proceed, they come together and commit themselves to one another, often in a ceremony in the presence of their family and friends. They declare that they will be committed to one another all the days of their lives and that they will forego similarly intimate relationships with persons other than their spouse.

When we commit ourselves to Christ, it is important to recognize that He has already committed Himself to us. He demonstrated His love towards each of us when He sacrificially died on the cross. In fact, the Bible says: "God has shown His love towards us in that while we were yet sinners, Christ died for us." Jesus tells us in the fifteenth chapter of John that there is no greater way that a person can demonstrate his love towards another person than to lay down his life for the person he loves. It is clear that Jesus waits for each of us. He stands committed to us, waiting patiently for our commitment to Him. The question remains "What will we do with Him?"

When a marriage ceremony is complete, the two people involved are publicly declared to be man and wife. Where moments before they were two single individuals, they now become a married couple. They are in a position to embark on a new and exciting life together in a marriage relationship.

Likewise, when a person commits his life to Jesus Christ, at that moment, he becomes a Christian. The barrier of sin has been broken as he stands before God, a forgiven sinner. He is now ready to embark on an exciting life in a relationship with God. If you will recall, in the second chapter, "A Purpose In Life," I introduced the idea that mankind comes into this world spiritually incomplete. He has a spiritual dimension and certain spiritual needs that must be attended to if he is ever to be fulfilled and spiritually complete. This is accomplished through an intimate personal relationship with God, who hungers for a relationship with all individuals. However, we should understand that a relationship with Him is impossible without a commitment in faith to His son Jesus Christ.

When I first considered this commitment, I was frightened by the prospect of being a Christian. I feared what God was going to do in my life, and I was concerned that He wanted to steal an enjoyable life away from me. Nevertheless, I recognized that I was spiritually dead and that though I seemed to be living the "good life" something was missing. One evening, I let go of my life and gave it to Jesus Christ.

That was eighteen years ago. As I look back, I can see how erroneous my preconceptions about God and the Christian life were. I have learned that God does not want to change my personality, but He does want to change my character. I have also learned that He requires excellence in all arenas of life. I can now declare with my whole heart that Jesus was speaking the truth when He said that He had not come as a thief to steal life away, but, rather, that he "came that you might have life and that you might have it abundantly."

The abundant life that Christ speaks of involves satisfying our deepest and innermost longings. This includes the need for love, security, joy, and meaning. Unfortunately, we so often seek satisfaction and truth in cheap counterfeits, believing them to be real life. It is hard for us to recognize that as we indulge ourselves more in the physical pleasures of life, the less these pleasures satisfy. The truth of the matter is that God's physical creation was intended for delight but not satisfaction. Only God can satisfy the human heart.

Rejecting Christ

Jesus made it clear that receiving Him in faith would result in the forgiveness of sin and the opportunity to have an eternal relationship with God. If this is true, then to reject him or to fail to act upon His initiation results in a failure to be forgiven. Jesus said that unless a person puts his faith in Him, "you shall die in your sins." (John 8:24) He goes on to say that such a failure results in a person being eternally separated from God. "He who believes in the Son has eternal life; but he who does not obey the Son shall not see life, but the wrath of God abides on Him." (John 3:36)

When Andrew Jackson was President of the United States, an employee in his administration was accused of murder. Due to the fact that the evidence was circumstantial, President Jackson pardoned him. The man refused the pardon and went to trial where he was found guilty and sentenced to be executed. A question arose over what to do with a condemned man who had refused a Presidential pardon. The matter went back to the court and it was determined that a pardon is no good unless the one to whom it has been given accepts it. He was therefore sent to his execution.

God has pardoned the whole world through the death of His Son Jesus Christ. However, this pardon is no good unless we as individuals receive Him by faith. We learn in the gospel according to John that as many as receive Him, to them He gives the right to be adopted into His family as Christians. (John 1:12)

The Difference God Makes

I once attended a friend's birthday party where most of those in attendance were upper middle class and quite successful professionally. We were completely at ease with one another and with the elegant setting of the party. One of the guests, however, stood out. His rumpled attire and unstudied appearance made me think that he might be some type of artist. As the party progressed, I looked for an opportunity to find out who this fellow was. I finally maneuvered myself into a position where I could introduce myself.

After a brief exchange of names, I asked the typical question: "What do you do?" I must admit that I was not prepared for his response. He told me that normally he made films but, at the present, he was in search of the truth. As we talked, I was excited about the direction the conversation was headed, for it opened the door for me to share with him what I believed to be the source of truth and where he might go to find it. He asked several questions and I told him that I was a Christian.

He responded to this with a question I had never been asked. "What kind of Christian are you?" After reflecting on the question, I responded that I was a Bible-believing Christian. This seemed to be a satisfactory answer for he listened with real interest and intensity to the ideas that I shared with him.

I have often reflected on that curious question—What kind of Christian are you? With all the media coverage that various churches and Christian ministries receive, it is no wonder that a person would ask "What kind of Christian are you?" Are you a fundamentalist, a charismatic, a Baptist, a Catholic, or an evangelical Christian—just what kind of Christian are you?

In America, we have seen and heard of so many people who have supposedly been converted or have had a religious experience that we become highly skeptical of the idea of "becoming a Christian." For many, it seems to be nothing more than a passing fancy that certain people experience. Nevertheless, something must happen when a person makes a complete about-face in his lifestyle and radically alters his values in order to follow Jesus Christ. The inquisitive soul asks, "Is this genuine? Is this for real?"

In closing, I would like to describe to you how God does, in fact, make a legitimate difference in people's lives. I shall do this by drawing upon a sampling of experiences related by several different people. As you read their life stories, ask yourself if the experiences of these individuals are true or are they only imagined.

A Will Greater Than Our Own

Peter Moore tells us the story of John, a college classmate of his who later became an architect, and how God introduced Himself into John's life. Here is how John describes the experience:

For twenty-five years I was a card-carrying member of the humanistic church, denying the existence of God, professing faith in man, and preaching the glories of the coming age, when men and women of both intellect and good will would govern a world flourishing under the application of scientific principles. Moreover, I was determined to be one of the leaders in that brave new world as, I thought, my eight years of undergraduate and graduate training at Yale had prepared me to be. Unbeknownst to me, however, was the presence of an invisible hand in my life with a will infinitely greater than mine and a plan for me very different from my own. Here is not the place to record all of its manifestations. One is relevant in this context.

I read voraciously; and it seemed that, in every book which I read, I encountered a piece of evidence or an argument which undermined the humanistic religion which I had adopted. Slowly at first, and then more rapidly, my views regarding natural history, human history, human nature, and the nature of human knowledge began to change. Eventually I was forced to admit the reality of God. The incredible design of the universe required the hand of an equally awesome architect. How strange that such an idea took twenty-five years to penetrate the mind of a member of my profession.

Because it is one of man's most ancient records, my studies in natural and human histories took me into the Old Testament. I became well acquainted with its contents; and my estimation of its accuracy rose with each successive visit. One day it occurred to me to ask myself, if the Old Testament is reasonably reliable, is the New Testament equally so? Little did I foresee the consequences of that query.

One spring morning in 1980, alone in my study, I was reading in the Gospel of John when I experienced something so dramatic that my life can be divided into the time before and the time after. I changed. . . . In the process of what happened, I acknowledged before God that I had sinned and did repent of my sins, that Jesus Christ is His Son and my Lord, and that he was entitled to my service for the rest of my life, regardless of the costs . . . . Until that day, I was blind to the spiritual world, but on that day, I glimpsed the Kingdom of God.

The Shining Promise of Life

One of the greatest literary geniuses of all times was the Russian author Leo Tolstoy. From a very early age, it was obvious that he was an exceptional talent. With an inherited estate and immediate literary success, the young Tolstoy found himself alternating between an ardent delight for social prosperity and fame and an equally passionate lust for women.

By the time he reached his mid-twenties, he had tired of the social life in Moscow, and found an escape by moving to the countryside with his beloved brother Nicholas, whose army battery was stationed there in Caucasus. This change of scenery he found to be marvelous, as he found the Cossack women entrancing and military life very much to his taste.

In many ways, Tolstoy found the military to have a certain appeal. It required courage, a quality he himself valued greatly, and it offered the opportunities of danger and risk along with opportunities for wild living which suited his temperament. However, it is ironic that though he enjoyed this life of excitement as a young man, it was during these years that he was driven to the conclusion that the reality of life was essentially spiritual.

Tolstoy was a man of incomparable gifts, with great wealth, a large family, a loving wife, every worldly blessing a person can possibly aspire to, and yet he found himself in total despair. In his *Confessions*, he admitted that when working in his study, he had to hide away a rope that was there for fear he would use it to hang himself. For Tolstoy, life had grown intolerable.

The one source of encouragement in his life was the community of old, uneducated Christian peasants in his town, whom he often found to be wiser and more in touch with the realities of our human existence than his educated aristocratic friends. Furthermore, he understood that the intellectual elite were horrified by the prospect of dying because they had seen no point to life other than in living it. However, the peasants confronted death with tranquility, content that their days should end and that they would be with the Lord.

It was at this time that Tolstoy turned to the Gospels in the New Testament and embraced the love of Jesus Christ, who spoke lucidly to him through each page of the scriptures. For Tolstoy, the dark menacing figure of death was transformed into the shining promise of life.

As Tolstoy wrote, "For thirty-five years of my life I was, in the proper acceptation of the word, a nihilist—not a revolutionary socialist, but a man who believed in nothing. Five years ago, my faith came to me. I believed in the doctrine of Jesus, and my whole life underwent a sudden transformation. Life and death ceased to be evil; instead of despair I tasted joy and happiness that death could not take away."

A Book That Understands

Peter Moore, in his book *Disarming The Secular Gods*, describes in a refreshing way how a young Frenchman, Emile Caulliet, became a Christian.

As a young French scholar in search of truth, he spent years studying the great philosophers and taking notes on their writings. After nearly a decade of this he read his notes and was profoundly disappointed. 'I shall write my own philosophy,' he said to himself and proceeded to do so. After another decade he reviewed his work. Again he was disappointed. He had that same empty feeling he got when he read the great philosophers.

Arriving at his home one day, Caulliet came upon his wife reading the Bible. "Get that book of superstition out of this house," he said. She refused and pleaded with him to give it at least a superficial glance. He agreed, reluctantly. But then he found that the more he read, the more engrossed he became in the text. In the end Caulliet became a convinced Christian and in time went on to spend many of his most creative years as a professor at Princeton Theological Seminary. He later described that fresh encounter with the Bible: "At last, I found a book which understands me!"

Not By Reason Alone

Blaise Pascal, the seventeenth-century philosopher, scientist, and mathematician found himself deeply concerned about and in combat with the rationalists of his day. Mistakenly they thought they could find truth through reason alone. Pascal knew that real humanity could never be found apart from God. Through the transforming process whereby his eyes were opened to God in Jesus Christ, Pascal came to the conclusion that while reason is a great servant it is a poor master. A loose translation of one of his better-known passages shows that he and the apostle John reflected on the same truths:

> To look only at God breeds pride; to look only at ourselves breeds despair. But when we find Jesus Christ we find our true equilibrium, for there we find not only God, but ourselves as well.

A Heart Opens To The Truth

Once again, Peter Moore strikes right at the heart of the issue of conversion and describes a most interesting encounter with a young man:

> By a unique series of circumstances in 1968 I found myself chaplain to the historic little Anglican parish of St. Peter's in Zermatt, Switzerland. In the predominantly English congregation one Sunday morning a face stood out. The young man had long, blond hair in the fashion of the sixties, and he was listening to

my sermon with the kind of intensity that is every preacher's wish. The sermon contrasted the hope of the gospel with the lack of hope found in contemporary culture. I felt it was too full of quotes from gloomy existentialist writers like Camus, Sartre, and Beckett. But it turned out that these were precisely the authors that this young man had been reading in search of answers to the fundamental questions of life.

Bob came to see me that afternoon in the little hotel where my wife and I were staying. For two hours he drilled me with questions about Christianity. He told me he had been president of S.D.S., the radical Students for a Democratic Society at Harvard in the sixties and had then dropped out of college following a bitter demonstration he led against the university in front of the president's house. The sudden and dramatic experience of power he felt as the leader of that demonstration precipitated an intellectual crisis within him during which he became aware that he had no basis for the values in which he so passionately believed. Once out of college he began heavy experimentation with drugs in an attempt to discover meaning in a world where there were just too few handles to grasp. Bob took off for Europe and based himself in Stockholm. For several months he backpacked and hitchhiked everywhere, spending his idle moments reading authors whose view of reality ended in absurdity and despair.

It was the church bells that morning and the desire to hear some English spoken that caused him to wander into St. Peter's. Our conversation that afternoon was only the beginning. Bob left Zermatt, went to the L'Abri community nearby at my suggestion and subsequently began reading the New Testament. But drawn though he was to real faith, doubts flooded through his mind as he sought to reconcile his agnostic assumptions with the answers he was hearing and reading.

Finally, he realized that he had been wanting God to convince him of the truth of Christianity before he decided to embrace it. From his "objective" perspective this all seemed quite reasonable. But he came to see that his unwillingness to submit to the truth (if it was so) was one of the main obstacles in the way of his ever discovering it. So late one night that spring he prayed: "Lord, if you're there, you can convince me that you're there. I don't know what it will take, but if you are truly God, you can do it. And, Lord, I know that I am supposed to pray, give my life to you and then follow you. I can't pray that. I'm not together enough to promise you my life . . . but if you are God, you can enable me to do that." Bob writes: "As I finished praying, there were no trumpets, no writing on the wall, just an incredible sense of peace and assurance that God was there. Since then I have had a real conviction that has never been shaken that Christianity is true."

Returning to Cambridge, Bob graduated, went to theological seminary, was ordained, ran a drug and alcohol agency for the State of Maryland, and then pursued public service as an elected representative in the state assembly. Bedrock to his life is the conviction that to understand the logic of the gospel, one's heart must be open to the truth.

A Reluctant Convert

One of England's most respected scholars, authors, and teachers was C. S. Lewis. Not only did he have great wit and imagination, he was an atheist and skeptic during the early years of his life. You can see his cynicism towards Christianity in a letter to his father in 1928: "There is a religious revival going on among our undergraduates . . . run by a Dr. Buchman. He gets a number of young men together and they confess their sins to one another. Jolly, ain't it? But what can you do? If you try to suppress it you only make martyrs."

Over the next two years, something began to happen in Lewis's life. In a letter to his friend Owen Barten, Lewis stated: "Terrible things are happening to me. The Spirit . . . is showing an alarming tendency to become much more personal and is taking the offensive, and behaving just like God."

It was not long after this that Lewis found his faith: "I had always wanted above all things, not to be interfered with. I had wanted to call my soul my own. I had been far more anxious to avoid suffering than to achieve delight. You must picture me alone in that room in Magdalen, night after night, feeling whenever my mind lifted even for a second from my work, the steady, unrelenting approach of Him whom I so earnestly desired not to meet. That which I greatly feared had at last come upon me. In the Trinity Term of 1929 I gave in, and admitted that God was God, and knelt and prayed: perhaps the most dejected and reluctant convert in all England."

C. S. Lewis went on to become one of the most prolific writers of Christian literature ever to have lived. His works have profoundly influenced men, women, and children throughout the twentieth century.

In Stillness and In Quiet

Here is the remarkable, the truly extraordinary story of Tom Nelson in his own words.

If ever a man has felt that he emerged from the womb gay, it is I. The sense of being "different," insecure, inadequate, and incomplete plagued me for years. Thoughts of homosexual orientation badgered me daily. Why? How, I would ask myself, could I be so disoriented in my sexuality and gender identity?

A self-imposed isolation soothed the pain of my confusion, yet it also inflicted the anguish of my loneliness. The prospect of significant peer relationships was dismal. Men appeared too cold, harsh, demanding, and insensitive—I was threatened by them; women seemed devouring and manipulative—I distrusted them. I viewed men as symbols of strength that I longed to become yet detested at the same time. This ambivalence toward men as well as toward women contributed to my increasing gender insecurity.

As time went by and I entered into my adolescent years my homosexual orientation became more pronounced. I became addicted to pornography, which afforded some temporary numbing of the inner pain. I discovered that bonding with pornographic images could serve as a form of anonymous sex that demanded no commitment to a relationship that might end in rejection or embarassment.

Then came the homosexual encounters, the actual acting out of my desires. However, I soon discovered that homosexual realtionships and homosexual sex would never prove to be the solution to my lack of masculine identity.

Finally, I sought to know Jesus as Lord. As I came to understand Him and His truths through His word, His kingdom, and His personal relation to me, I found the sense of identity, security, and wholeness that I had so longed for. I learned that I did not constantly have to strive for acceptance. Jesus Christ had always accepted me unconditionally. Through seeking above all else His kingdom and His righteousness (Matthew. 6:33) I was able to begin reconstructing my old, faulty notions of man, woman, father, mother, authority, and even God Himself.

My gender insecurity diminished as I examined and embraced my masculine traits. Confidence and assertiveness began to overpower inadequacy and "wimpiness." The fire of attraction for men dwindled. Pornography's strong grip, a separate battle, also saw its death.

The deeply rooted heterosexual identity planted within by the Creator had finally emerged! I no longer had the insurmountable fear of dating women. Gone was the repulsion to marriage and heterosexual relationships. After years of asking God to prepare me for my wife and her for me, my faith was finally manifested in the reality of marriage, God's sanctioned union. Marriage was the catalyst for the final stage of my healing and restoration.

Sure, there were countless times I wanted to abandon the struggle. Often I thought, "This just isn't worth the pain." However, God's merciful love and abundant grace escorted me through the whole process. All I needed was to completely surrender myself— all my hurt, confusion, and misperception—to Him. Then, in stillness and in quiet, I received His good gifts of true life and freedom. In Him, I found my true self.

A Golden Opportunity

There is probably no greater example of a family experiencing the American Dream than the Adolph Coors family of Golden, Colorado. It is one of the great success stories in the history of American business.

As a German immigrant, Adolph Coors, Sr. came to America just after the Civil War and worked in a local Brewery in Denver, Colorado. He was a hard-working man who believed that in order to achieve success, you never give up. One day in 1873, he made a discovery that would change the course of his life. As he was traveling on foot from Denver to Golden, Colorado, (where the Coors Brewery sits today), he noticed water bubbling up from the ground. As a trained brewer, he knew water was the key ingredient in making good beer. Upon sampling the water he knew that it was perfect for the production of beer.

Coors took a partner and purchased an old tannery building in Golden and formed what came to be known as the Golden Brewery. He threw himself into the business. In 1880, he bought out his partner and formed the Adolph Coors company. The company flourished and grew.

Both Adolph Coors, Jr. and Adolph Coors, III followed in the footsteps of the their patriarch, totally committed to the family business.

As chairman of the board of the company, Adolph Coors, III continued to expand the business as the family's wealth multiplied. He was also one of the early founders and directors of the Aspen Ski Company in Aspen, Colorado.

His son, Adolph Coors, IV, remembers him as a powerful man, yet a loving father who spent quality time with his family. He provided them with everything money could buy. Though his father had no spiritual life, he made sure that his children were dropped off at church on Sunday, that they might find God on their own.

In 1958, Coors III moved his family from Denver to their dream home on a ranch just outside of Morrison, Colorado. On February 9, 1960, he left his home early in the morning while his family still slept, and began his drive to the brewery. It was a cold morning, and as he was nearing the brewery, he noticed a yellow car that appeared to be broken down on a bridge that he was to cross. As Coors got out of his car to assist the stranded pedestrian, he was confronted by Joseph Corbett, who had staged this scene in an attempt to kidnap the wealthy businessman. A struggle ensued and as Coors staggered back to his car he was shot several times in the back and he died. Corbett stuffed the body in the trunk and headed south.

The disappearance of Coors III made national headlines as authorities searched diligently for the missing business magnate. It was not until months later that the remains of his body were found in a garbage dump near Denver.

During those months that his father was missing, young Adolph Coors IV prayed that God would return his father to their family. When the body was found, the young Coors concluded that God must not exist.

From this point forward, the Coors family began to unravel. Mrs. Coors III had become an alcoholic and was not strong enough to cope with life now that her husband was gone. The relationships between all the family members became strained.

The young Adolph Coors felt deserted by everyone as no one came forward to comfort him in his grief. He was expected to be a man and to be strong. Nevertheless, he continually looked for ways to relieve the pain and loneliness in his heart. He fared poorly as a student and consequently began to hate himself for he believed that he did not measure up to the Coors' name.

After three years of military service, he returned to Colorado and married his high school sweetheart. With all of his inherited wealth he and his new wife began a journey in which they were convinced that money could purchase a happy life. After several years of riotous living, attempting to stay on the fast track at the brewery, and watching his marriage fall apart, young Adolph Coors, IV realized his life was in shambles. To make matters worse, a crippling automobile accident forced him to leave the brewery. He was thus faced with the prospect of never amounting to anything.

It was at this time that a vice president at the brewery came to visit him and his wife. He began to share with them the claims of Jesus Christ. Coors' wife, B. J., gave her life to Christ. Six months later, in June of 1975, at the age of thirty, Adolph Coors, IV, cried out to God, and surrendered his life to Christ, asking that He put his life back together.

Life for the Coors family has not been the same since that day. Their priorities changed and they began to rebuild their marriage. They both experienced a fulfillment and sense of purpose that their previous life could not produce.

There was only one lingering problem. Adolph Coors, IV had cultivated a hatred towards Joseph Corbett (who had been caught and sentenced to life in prison). He was not able to let go of it. One day, a friend challenged him to go to the Colorado State Penitentiary and face Corbett. Though he resisted at first, he knew it had to be done if he was going to really live again. Though Corbett would not see him, he left the prisoner a Bible and a personal letter. In that letter, he asked Corbett to forgive him for all the hatred he carried with him since that fateful day. Coors also told him that that he and his family had forgiven him for all the grief and heartache he had caused. As Coors walked out of the prison he realized he was a free man.

Today, Adolph Coors, IV will tell you that the miraculous transformation and healing that has taken place in his life, was not the result of organized religion, but from a personal relationship with Jesus Christ.

A Chinese Miracle

Larry Burkett, a nationally respected business and financial consultant, shares the story of a humble Chinese immigrant.

A few years ago, a business associate who had recently returned from China asked me to have lunch with him. When I arrived, he had another fellow with him who was obviously Oriental. With involuntary habit, I sized him up to be poor, since he was wearing a suit made for a man two sizes larger, and he had very bad posture (stooped back). As we sat down to eat, I noticed that this little man was typically "old-world" Oriental. He smiled almost constantly, said "Yes, sir" and "No, sir" to me even though he was obviously more than twice my age, and he steadfastly refused to eat a "normal" American portion of food.

He spoke broken English but seemed to understand it quite well, and as the meal progressed, I began to ask about him with my friend interpreting. He was Chinese, a Christian for more than thirty years, and a traveling evangelist in China (he walked). In the late 1940s, he fought with Mao Tse-tung's Communist army against Chiang Kai-shek's army, and when Mao took over he was a well-positioned Communist official. To rid the country of "dissidents," Mao sent execution squads throughout China. On the "hitlist" were noncommunist officials, school teachers, those with relatives in the West, undesirables, and especially Christians, since they were opposed to atheism.

This little man was directly responsible for more than 10,000 executions during the first year of Communist rule. (It is estimated that the Communists executed 25,000,000 people during the first decade of Mao's reign). While traveling from village to village executing the "dissidents," he and his squad came across a man transporting manure to a community garden. When asked who the leader of the community was, the man replied, "I am, sir." Well, a good Communist wasn't about to believe that. He had seen that what Lenin taught was true—under the old Chinese feudal system "leaders" always exploited the masses and Communism was the system to correct that wrong. The Communist leader said, "Even in our perfect system (Communism), leaders do not handle manure; that is a servant's job." To which the man replied, "Here we do, sir, for this is a Christian community and the Bible says that God's leader is the servant of others."

This so startled the Communist that he forgot to shoot the man. The only place he had ever heard such radical talk from a leader was in the "Party" before they took over. After they took over, such notions were the "ideal" but would have to be delayed until their "enemies" were defeated. Oh yes, he had heard such ideals taught in church before the war, but it was always from someone who didn't practice what he preached and who was living far better than most of his congregation. So, rather than execute this group, he decided to stay and observe them to expose their lies. A few weeks later, after he observed the small community of believers who were as committed to living out their beliefs as the Communists were to dying for theirs, he accepted Jesus Christ as his Savior. The Christians shared their food with other villages whose adult populations had been wiped out during the war; they adopted hundreds of orphan kids; they even prayed daily for the Communists who had passed laws making public prayer a capital offense.

The little man headed back to Peking to share the truth of Christ with his former comrades, and he was instantly jailed and put on trial for his life. In court he witnessed to all who would listen until his mouth was sewn shut. His defection from the party so infuriated the leadership that they made him a "project" to reconvert to communism. He was offered his freedom and a pardon if he would denounce Christ and swear allegiance to Mao, but he steadfastly refused. Over the next few years his wife, children, and every relative were executed in retaliation for his "treachery." He was beaten almost every day, starved, and had his back broken at least twice (which accounted for his bad posture). He virtually memorized the Bible over the next twenty years in prison in solitary confinement by smuggled-in scraps of paper with Scriptures written on them.

He was released in the late 1970s as China once again tried to improve relations with the West. Almost immediately he set out across China to share his faith with everyone who would listen. He literally went out with nothing except some cheap clothing given to him by other believers. A few years later he met my friend, who was doing business in inland China, and was asked to visit the U.S. to help raise money to purchase Bibles for China.

Since that day, this uneducated ex-murderer who never owned more than one ill-fitting suit has passed away. My friend said every time he gave the Chinese preacher extra money for a better suit the Chinese always found someone more needy than he and gave it away. This much I do know. . . he was considerably closer to the truth of God's Word than most of us are . . . including me.

The Living Reality of Christ

Dan Hayes, a lecturer and author with the Campus Crusade organization shares an encounter he had with a young woman who attended one of his lectures on Christianity at Oklahoma State University. When his lecture had ended, he noticed a young woman waiting for the audience to empty so that she could speak with him. She finally approached him and explained that she wanted to talk with him alone because she was different from the other students that were in attendance. She then explained that she was Jewish, and that her father was a rabbi. She told him that she had just spent a year in Israel trying to discover what is real in this life. However, she was dejected over what she had witnessed. The Jews hated the Palestinians, the Palestinians hated the Jews, and, she confessed, she could not find any love at all there. Consequently, she returned to her home in Irvine, California, and she confided that even among her family and friends there was nothing but backbiting and arguing. She therefore decided to return to school though she really did not know why.

She said to Dan, "You spoke of Jesus Christ as though He was knowable and I could experience His love."

Dan responded, "You certainly can. Would you like to talk about it?"

For the next hour or two, they went through the Old Testament and looked at the great prophecies concerning Christ because this was naturally of great interest to her. However, the question that plagued her was, "Can I and will I experience His love?"

Five weeks later he received a letter from her.

"Dear Dan, after considering what you said and after considering the New and Old Testaments, I have decided to give Jesus Christ the position as Lord, Savior, and Messiah of my life. You said I could experience Christ and His love and you were absolutely right. I have begun to pray to Him and I have found He is always there and He has truly become a living reality in my life."

Reflections of A Former Skeptic

One of the world's most eloquent and inspiring journalists of the twentieth century was Great Britain's Malcolm Muggeridge. For many years a fierce and determined skeptic, Muggeridge eventually was lead to embrace the Christian faith. Reflecting on his life and accomplishments, Muggeridge said:

> I may, I suppose, regard myself, or pass for being a relatively successful man. People occasionally stare at me in the streets—that's fame. I can fairly easily earn enough to qualify for admission to the higher slopes of the Internal Revenue—that's success. Furnished with money and a little fame even the elderly, if they care to, may partake of trendy diversions—that's pleasure. It might happen once in a while that something I said or wrote was sufficiently heeded for me to persuade myself that it represented a serious impact on our time—that's fulfillment. Yet I say to you— and I beg you believe me—multiply these tiny triumphs by a million, add them all together, and they are nothing—less than nothing, a positive impediment—measured against one draught of that living water Christ offers to the spiritually thirsty, irrespective of who or what they are.

When Muggeridge was in his eighties, recognizing that his life was coming to a conclusion, he shared his thoughts on death. "The worst news anybody could give to me now is that they have found a medication that would give me fifteen more years to live. I do not want to live any longer, for I have lived long enough. I can hardly wait to go on and meet the Lord." Seven months later, he received the desire of his heart.

REMEMBERING THE FORGOTTEN GOD

The Search For Truth In The Modern World

Joseph Jennings, a young black man, was determined to free himself from the inner city poverty into which he was born. He reasoned that the only way to escape the indignities of racism and despair would be to make as much money as he could in the shortest period of time—which meant he would have to break the law by selling drugs. Eventually, he reached his twisted goals and did, in fact, move up in the world. But, he tells us, something critical remained absent from his life.

One hot summer day, Byron Payne, my uncle from Indiana who had moved to California, knocked on my door. He had driven past an antique car dealership and seen a Rolls Royce that was awesome. I said, "Let's go check it out." When we walked in, the sales person treated us like nobodies. He seemed to think that we weren't the type for this class of car—I developed an immediate hatred for him.

I left there determined to return. In two weeks, when my next drug deal was completed, I walked back into the dealership just before closing. I was met by the same sales clerk. He became very nervous. I went over to his desk and threw down all the cash needed to buy the Rolls Royce. Then I arrogantly told him to give me the keys to my car. He stuttered, 'Y-Y-Yes, sir,' as he counted the money and put it into the safe. He must have thought I was going to rob him, because he murmured that the safe had a time lock on it. I just laughed.

I had a new toy. A piece of the American Dream. At that point in my life my dealings in southern California had gotten so big that I could afford anything I wanted. I had a 3,000 square foot home with a swimming pool and jacuzzi. I had gold jewelry, clothes and lots of money to buy anything else I desired.

I had begun to make many friends in the film and music industry in Los Angeles and made regular trips there for parties, visits and drug drop-offs. My life at this point seemed to be one party after another, but the paranoia was becoming intense. I felt perhaps it was time to cool down and get some of the heat off me. I was lonely and very anxious to be with my children again. I had them relocated to California to live.

I began to spend more time with them. I was going to give them everything I never had, the things I only dreamed of at their age. The next month was April and my two oldest sons, Joseph Jr. and James, both had birthdays that month. I arranged a catered party on a yacht off an island in California. I sent stretch limousines to pick up their friends. They danced, ate and partied. Afterwards I took them to my home to swim all night.

I thought by doing these things I was being a good father.

So much flash. So much glitter. So much money. So much loneliness. So much emptiness.

In the process of realizing the American Dream—in his efforts "to be somebody"—Joseph Jennings was shot thirteen times and suffered multiple stab wounds. He was arrested on more than one occasion and eventually became addicted to cocaine. He did it all before coming to the realization that what he was really seeking was simply the truth.

You shall know the truth and the truth shall set you free. Therefore, if the son makes you free, you shall be free indeed. (John 8:32-36)

Joseph Jennings tells us that when he first read these words "my heart seemed to explode with joy. I fell to the ground as I heard the Lord giving me a personal invitation. I cried out to Him in surrender and rejected the way I had been living. I confessed my sins and asked for His forgiveness."

• • • •

God has given each and every one of us a free will so that we can make our own choices in life. You can either choose to give your life to Him through faith in Jesus Christ, or you can reject Him and choose to go your own way. For the person who chooses for Christ, all that is required is a commitment from the heart.

A Commitment From The Heart
(A Closing Prayer)

Lord, I acknowledge that I have tried to live life my way. I now recognize that by charting my own course, I have disregarded Your desires for my life. I have pretended to be self-sufficient, not needing forgiveness or direction. I have forgotten You.

Because I am human, I am sinful. I need the forgiveness that only Christ can offer. I submit my life to You completely, and it is truly my desire to follow You, now and forever.

Amen

Does a blind man believe in sunsets because he has seen one or because he trusts the testimony of the people he respects who have seen one, the logic of their arguments for its existence, and their emotional communication of its beauty and majesty?

Unknown

Notes

Introduction

1. A Shattered Visage by Ravi Zacharias, Wolgemuth & Hyatt Publishers, 1990, page 12.
2. Sermon BY Ravi Zacharias, "Why I am not an Atheist."

The Existence of God

1. What Americans Believe by George Barna
2. Whatever Happened to the Human Race by Francis Schaffer, Fleming H. Revell Co., 1978, page 137.
3. Idols for Destruction, by Herbert Schlossberg, Thomas Nelson Publishers, 1983, pages 171 and 172.
4. "Christian Fianancial Concepts," by Larry Burkett, interview with Charles Colson, September 15, 1989.
5. Idols For Destruction, ibid, page 149.
6. ?
7. ?
8.In Search of Dignity by R.C. Sproul, Regal Books, 1983, pages 98

and 99.

9. Twilight of a Great Civilization, by Carl Henry, Corssway Books, 1988, page 159.

10.?

11.?

12. Waking From The American Dream by Donald McCullough, Intervarsity Press, 1988, page 102.

13?

14. Imprimis by William Kirkpatrick, Spring 1986.

15. Christianity of Trial, by Colin Chaopman, Tyndale ouse Pu8blishers, 1974, pages 295 and 296.

16. How To Be Your Own Selfish Pig by Susan Schaeffer Macaulay, Chariot Books, 1986, pages 81 and 82.

17. The Intellectuals Speak Out About God, edited by Roy Abraham Varghese, written by Norman Geisler, Published by Regnery GAteway, Inc., pages 147 and 148.

18. How Should We Then Live by Francis Schaeffer, Fleming Revell Company, 1976, page 180.

19.

20.

21.Me, Myself, and Who by Ernest Gordon, Logos International, 1980, page 110.

A Purpose In Life

1. Interview with Woody Allen, Esquire Magazine, May 1977.

2. The Rest of Success by Denis Haack, Intervarsity Press, 1989, pages 51 and 52.

3. Me, Myself, and Who, op cit, pages 63 and 64.

4.A Shattered Visage, op cit, pages 87 and 89.

5. Time Magazine, January 8, 1990.

6. Kingdoms in Conflict by Charles Colson, Zondervan Publishing, 1987, page 68.

7. Ordering Your Private World by Gordon MacDonald, Thomas Nelson Publishers, page 115.

8. Mere Christianity by C.S. Lewis, Macmillan Publishering, 1943, page 43.

Does God Have A Name?

1. The Dust of Death by Os Guinness, Intervarsity Press, 1973, page 340.

2. Jesus by Malcolm Muggeridge, Harper and Row Publishers, 1975, page 16.

3. Whi I Believe by D. James Kennedy, Word Publishing, 1980, page 97.

4. He Walked Among Us, by Josh McDowell, Here's Life Publishers, 1988, page 195.

5. Ibid.

6. ?

7. U.S. News & World Report, April 16, 1990, The Last Days of Jesus, page 53.

8. Evidence That Demands A Verdict, by Josh McDowell, Here's Life Publishers, 1972, page 183.

9. Disarming The SEcular Gods by Peter C. Moore, Intervarwsity Press, 1989, page 148.

10. Loving God by Charles Colson, Zondervan Books, 1983, pages 67 and 69.

11. Evidence That Demands A VErdict, op cit., page 192.

12. Ibid, 191.

13. Ibid, 190.

14. Why I Believe, op cit, 102.

15. Ibid

16. Evidence That Demands A Verdict, op cit, page 129.

17. Ibid, page 128.

18. Disarming The Secular Gods, page 102.

19. Mere Christianity, page 45.

20. Evidence That Demands A Verdict, op cit, pages 132 & 133.

21. ?

22. Evidence 128

23. Evidence 132

24.

25. The End of Christendom by Malcolm Muggeridge, William Eerdmans Publishing Company, 1980, pages 49 and 50.

The Condition of Man

1. Against The Night by Chgarles Colson, Servant Publications, 1989, pages 64 and 65.

2. Twilight of a Great Civilization by Carl Henry, Crossway Books, 1988, page 15

3. The Republic of Plato, Oxford University Press, 1945, page 45.

4. How Should We Then Live, page 78.

5. ??

6. Idols For Destruction, page 2.

7.

8. How Should We Then Live?, pages 208 and 209.

9. The Closing of The American Mind by Allen Bllom, Simon & Shuster, 1987, pages 25 to 43.

10. Why America Doesn't Work by Charles Colson and Jack Eckerd, Word Publishin, 1991, page 66.

11. Against The Night, Colson, page 82.

12. Twilight of a Great Civiliation, pages 170.

13.

14. Main Currents In Modern Thought by Hohn Hallowell.

16.??

17. I have this one (

Is The Bible Valid?

1. Disarming The Secular Gods, page 108.

2. Disappointment with God by Philip Yancy, Zondervan Publishing House, 1988. page

3. Evidence that Demands a Verdict, page 65.

4. Evidence that Demands a Verdict, page 66.

5.

6. Evidence That Demands A Verdict, page 66.

7. Evidence That Demands A Verdict, page 71.

8. Why I Believe, page 33.

9.Evidence That Demands A Verdict, page 82.

10.Evidence That Demands A Verdict, page 57 to 58.

11. Reason Enough by Clark Pinnock, Intervarsity Pres, 1980, page 76.

12. Evidence That Demands A Verdict, pages 42 and 43.

13. Evidence That Demands A Verdict, pages 42 and 43.

14.

The Barriers To Belief

1. The Road Less Traveled by M. Scott Peck, Simon and Schuster, 1978, pages 16 and 17.

2.

3. Idols For Destrucktion, pages 301.

4. Encyclopeia Americana, International Edition by Grolier Incorporated, 1985.
5. Encyclopedia Britannica, University of Chicago, 1985.
6. Lecture by Ron Carlson, "The Uniqueness of Jesus Christ in a World of Religions."
7. Christianity Today, "Good Pagans and God's Kingdom" by James I Packer, January 17, 1986, pages 22 to 25.
8. The Quest For Faith, by C. Stephen Evans, Intervarsity Press, 1986, page 133.

The Heart Of Christianity

1. The Enduring Question, Main Problems of Philosophy by Melvin Rader, Holt, Rinehart, and Winston, 1969, page 49.
2. Disarming The Secular Gods, page 83 & 84.
3. A Third Testament by Malcolm Muggeridge, Ballantine Books, 1976, page 145-170.
4. Disarming The Secular Gods, page 208.
5.
6. DisarmingThe Secluar Gods, pages 152 to 154.
7. Evidence That Demands a Verdict, pages 355 and 366.
8. This cam from a speech by Adolph Coors on his own life, "Mr Father's Son."
9.
10. Lecture by Dan Hayes on Prayer
11. Jesus Rediscovered by Malcolm Muggeridge, Doubleday 1969, pages 77 and 78.
12. Jennings Book

Acknowledgments

I am grateful to Bobby Frese and Rob Pearigen who contributed significantly to the editing of this book, particularly in its early stages. I also would like to thank Phil Reddick, Tommy Brigham, Jane Geiger, and Charles and M. J. Bagby for their critique and encouragement in this endeavor. I would also like to thank Jane Major and Cam Bullock for their editorial skills and sharp eyes in copyediting and proofreading the final pages. And Jocelyn Bradley and Leigh Ann Roberts for their kind and constructive words of support.

I would be remiss if I did not acknowledge those individuals whose work has greatly influenced my life and consequently has shaped the substance of this book. To Charles Colson, whose books, articles, and speeches have profoundly shaped my thinking and my perspective on life. The works of Dr. Francis Schaffer and Josh McDowell have provided the basis for my intellectual foundation and defense of the Christian faith. Josh McDowell's tremendously powerful book *Evidence that Demands a Verdict* which I first read in 1975, encouraged my renewed commitment to Christ and helped me to realize that Christianity is intellectually defensible. I am grateful to Ravi Zacharias and his lectures, which influenced this work and continue to affect my spiritual life. Herb Schallsburg's wonderful book *Idols for Destruction* was a most important resource in my research. I must also express my thanks and appreciation to Dr. Peter Moore for the use of the material I quoted from his book, *Disarming the Secular Gods.* I am appreciative of Phil Yancy, for his enlightened perspectives and the role his writings have played in my life and in this work. Finally, I cannot adequatedly express the appreciation and gratitude that should be given to the late Malcolm Muggeridge and C. S. Lewis, whose works have informed and molded not only my life and this book, but thousands of others throughout the world.

Collophon